My Crazy, Pregnant Wife!

An outrageous spin on pregnancy for dads!

A humorous, week-by-week playbook of surviving
pregnancy with your wife.

Jeff Walter

My Crazy, Pregnant Wife!

ISBN: 978-0-557-48583-3

June 2010; Jeff Walter

This book is dedicated to my wife, Ellen, who embraces our love and laughter in our marriage, three wonderful children, and the brief, yet cherished moments that we have together alone!

My Crazy, Pregnant Wife!

An outrageous spin on pregnancy for dads!

Prologue

When I decided to write this, my first thoughts were to rip into my wife and the nine months of torture that she was about to put me through. Don't get me wrong, the love and joy of sharing the experience of having a baby together is a beautiful thing. Yet, your wife, like mine, is going to transform into an emotional roller coaster that even the biggest thrill seeker will be begging to get the hell off of.

This book was written to provide an extreme and irreverent look at how we as husbands feel, yet rarely--or very delicately--express to our spouses. You are about to embark down a road that only your wife thinks she truly knows – pregnancy. You can try and relate, be sympathetic, and listen...but overall, your wife will constantly remind you of one thing – you don't know jack about being pregnant!

This indispensable resource taps directly into my weekly log of pregnant wife hysteria. It's here where the maternal magic begins. I've assigned a wife moodiness rating called the "Preggo-Stat." It's much like a thermostat that determines the temperature at a given moment, yet it determines the craziness of your wife as she nears her due date. This rating of LOW, MEDIUM, or HIGH will alert you as to how moody your wife will be in any given week of pregnancy. This insider information cluing you into her escalating hormone levels will lead you down the path of least resistance and potential peace during the otherwise hellacious months while you're living with your crazy pregnant wife.

Contents

My Crazy, Pregnant Wife!

Introduction

I love my wife. We have a wonderful relationship. Lately, she's gone a bit off the deep end...morning sickness, puking in the sink, stomach pains, headaches, nausea, the constant need to take a nap, and continuous complaints about how her clothes don't fit, or how she's fat and not the sexy vixen she was once before. Not pretty thoughts. Yet she's actually very attractive with that preggo belly.

At the same time, what about the changes I would go through? What about all the stuff that I was going to encounter when confronted with her emotions, yet still be required to completely understand, respect, even embrace, what my wife's body was adapting to?

Why was I feeling so distracted this time around? I've already been down this road twice, yet with our third pregnancy, I began to reflect about the next nine months in a darker way. As I paused to think about this, I remembered something from our first pregnancy that my wife yelled out to me while in labor: "You did this to me, and next time, you can have the baby!" Wow - that wasn't quite what I was expecting on our special day. At that point, I remembered one key piece of information.

As a man, I will never understand what it's like to be pregnant. No matter how much I would put into this next nine months, I still wouldn't get it. It's not my body; it's hers. She's the glorious temple that was chosen to carry this baby, and not me. At that moment, I relaxed a bit. Yes, she would have this special bond over the next nine months, and I wouldn't. My job would be simply to support her, love her, listen, and tend to her every need, regardless of how absurd I might think it is. Yes, you'll be your wife's slave for the next nine months. Get used to it. Almost every man goes through it – it's part of joining the club - kind of a right of passage. And you'll be able to share this wonderful nine-month experience with other new dads down the road.

Each pregnancy we've had has brought with it widely different emotions and expectations. Our first pregnancy was typical.

Every day wasn't complete without writing down some thoughts in the baby journal, posting online the weekly development of our baby, and reading numerous books about becoming parents. We went through 20 different paint pallets for the nursery, browsed baby stores every weekend for the perfect crib and matching changing table - which at the time cost more than all of the furniture in our master bedroom, combined! We spent weekends at baby stores buying just the right blankets and bedding that our bundle of joy would soon puke and pee all over. It was our first baby, our love, our soon to be new addition to the family.

Once our baby was born, she was and still is the most precious little girl we could ever ask for. The tears ran down my face, and I was forever a changed man holding this delicate new life in my arms. We took endless amounts of pictures, documented every week with our video camera, and officially joined the parenting club. This club is a special club, and it entitles you to share your best moments as parents, yet also allows you to vent about how you can't do anything that you used to do as a couple now that you are parents.

The second time around, the pregnancy was a bit on the "lighter" side. While we had many of the same feelings and dove into the same baby books as before, we seemed to get to things a bit later and then hastier. We chose the paint color much more quickly, pulled the old baby furniture back out of the attic, were given many clothes from other friends, and really didn't finish up the nursery until the week or two before our infant son was born.

While we experienced the excitement of having a boy this time around, we were still tending to the needs of our first child, which often distracted us from every detail of our new baby boy. Yet, the pregnancy still entitled my wife to the same benefits as before...naps, naps, and more naps, while I did the dishes, cooked, and re-stocked ice cream bars in the freezer as rapidly as she could eat them.

Yes, I was still stuck in the same role as the loving, supportive husband, while also serving as her towel boy and male servant on the side. This book is for any man going through a pregnancy with his lovely wife...whether it's your first, second, or sixth baby. Amidst all the pain, angst, and sleepless nights, you might be surprised to know that I wrote this book to bring out the humor of pregnancy from a guy's perspective. As I opened with, I love my wife dearly, and recognize that her body is going through something amazing that requires the physical and emotional strength that I will never encounter. I also know that she can eat 4 slices of pizza, 2 bowls of ice cream, and down a 32-ounce jug of water in 3 minutes. Yes, her body is going through something amazing and sometimes I'm not sure if there's going to be room for the baby in there!

40 Crazy Weeks

Weeks 1, 2, 3, 4

Fertilize that Egg

I spent the larger part of my life trying not to get a girl pregnant. From as far back as 8th grade, I remember sitting in health class discussing the penis and the vagina. As my health teacher explained (funny how it was always a coach that taught health class) how the penis and vagina come together and thus start the process of making a baby. I remember him standing in front of the class with a watering can. He then started to pour the water onto a few seeds in a flowerpot and asked us to visualize these seeds growing into a flower. How beautiful. This was how a 6' 6" basketball coach, aka health teacher, explained the beauty of procreation.

Ninth grade brought a whole new discussion into play. In today's school environment, this discussion should probably be taught in 6th grade. Anyway, 9th grade became a story of how not to water the seeds and how not to grow the beautiful flower. We were scared to death by our health teacher's explanation that sex would lead to pregnancy and we'd all be screwed – literally.

I'm sure we all remember our respective health teacher pulling out the banana and rolling down a condom around it. I sure can. My teacher used an extremely large banana for the demonstration, and as he maneuvered the condom around it, I think some of the girls in the class were getting aroused. As for us boys, we were in banana envy. I think our teacher should have gone with one of those smaller Brazilian bananas or maybe an early-stage carrot of some kind. It would have made me feel a bit better about myself.

That health class made many of us so uncomfortable that we were afraid of sex and getting a girl pregnant. Sure, I wanted to have sex, but I was scared to death about the whole thing. If I knew what I know now, I would have made oral sex more of a priority, since as a married man this is a seldom event, at best. But as a youth, I practiced rolling down the condom so that I would be ready when the time came. I even practiced putting on two sometimes.

My parents were pretty lax on the sex talk. I can remember a quick conversation that my mom had with me, and my dad sat me down once as well. It went like this: "Don't have sex, you could get a girl pregnant. Then you won't be able to go to college." I have to grant that this short speech was a lot easier on me than the banana demonstration.

Yet now I was spending the better part of my married nights trying to get a woman pregnant. What the hell. And when I want to pull out the watering can and water the seeds, it's not happening. Again, what the hell. There's nothing like having a lot of sex to get pregnant, yet eventually you'd like to get into the playoffs and score a goal in the big game.

Our first child, however, happened right away. Our second took three months. Our third, took five months. Whatever the case may be for you, enjoy the ride. Practicing for the big game is fun. No matter how long it takes, seize every opportunity.

Preggo-Stat temperature: MEDIUM

A mood swing this early in a potential pregnancy is more likely related to missing her period. Use your normal tactics for battling this moodiness. Only speak when spoken to. At some point in this week, your wife might take a pregnancy test. For the best results, wait until the latter part of the week. If the results are negative, take another one in week five. If results are positive, call your doctor, set up an appointment, and discuss what steps to take next for the health of your wife and baby.

Week 5

Pregnant, Let the Games Begin

Monday afternoon, my wife had arranged for a sitter to watch our two kids, ages three and five, while we went to dinner alone. My wife gave me a call at work and asked if I could meet her at one of our favorite Chinese restaurants, and I agreed. We had been trying for a few months now with no results. A nice, quiet dinner with my wife was just what I needed.

After we met at the restaurant, we talked for a bit outside while we waited for our table. She reached into her bag and pulled out a picture of our two kids. After looking at the picture for a few seconds, I realized that the kids had on some shirts with sayings on them. My daughter's shirt read, "Big Sister." This made sense, as she has a little brother. But my son's shirt read, "Big Brother." Now, that didn't make sense. My wife smiled at me and said, "Are you ready for the next nine months?" Wow – we did it! I couldn't believe it. It was just as exciting as the first time!

I was blown away and the biggest smile filled my face. My wife hugged me and we fought to hold back the tears. Another baby – this would be our last. We were going to embrace every moment of knowing that this would be the last time we'd be down this road. The next nine months will be the last nine-month adventure of this sort.

While this opens up a new chapter in our lives, it will eventually close three chapters of our lives - the birth of our three kids. This will be the last time I set up the crib and changing table in the nursery. This will be the last time we pick out little baby clothes and look at those tiny diapers. This will be nine months of last times, yet also new beginnings. This will also be the last time I change poopy diapers at 3 a.m. in the morning!

Preggo-Stat temperature: LOW

She's too excited to go crazy on you yet. She may begin to have fatigue, urinate more frequently, and feel nauseous. Encourage her to exercise (you too), as it will help prepare her for the physical parts of labor. Exercise is also a great stress reducer for any additional anxiety that may be brought upon the two of you over the next nine months.

Week 6

Your Pain is My Pain

Recently, my wife tends to be calling me more often at work to walk me through her cramps and pains, which the conversation always ending with a long moan clamoring for sympathy. Her stomachaches in the morning, and later the bloating begins after lunch. She can recall the exact number of times she's spit up in the sink and is more than willing to explain every gross detail. She then reminds me of how lucky I am that I don't have to go through this every day.

Somehow, she doesn't see that, yes, I actually am going through this every day...with her! Every freakin' day she walks me through the gas, burps, spit ups, and morning sickness. I would like to say, "Hey, could you keep it down in there, I'm trying to sleep."

Or maybe, "Yes, I know your feeling sick, but remember it's a privilege to have a baby and many women would be green with envy to be in your shoes." But then I'm reminded that I need to be the supporting husband and listen. "Yes honey. I wish there was more I could do for you." Men are problem solvers. We are not the best listeners. I process your need of being sick as needing some kind of medicine to resolve the ill feeling. My wife is not looking for that. We as men must constantly remind ourselves that we would be so much better off if we shut our mouths and just listened.

My wife has never been a morning person. When she had a career before our kids, she got up because she had to. When the weekends came around, I was lucky to see her out of bed and downstairs by 11 a.m. She'd still be in her robe, pajamas, and fuzzy bunny slippers looking for a jolt of coffee to wake her up. She has no desire to wake up at 6 a.m., read the paper, make a big breakfast, and get an early start on the day. I, on the other-hand, like to get up early, make coffee, have a big breakfast, and log in an early round of golf on the weekend. This all changes once baby arrives.

First of all, if your household is anything like what I've described so far, quickly change your habits. While you are a team and you're both going to be accepting changes in your life, one spouse starts to keep score a bit more intensely when it comes to personal time. Your early round of golf will be a no go. Your early morning run, exercise at the gym, set of tennis, or whatever you may be up to on the weekends, will disappear. Your personal life and hobbies will now be dictated by baby, your wife's schedule, and your wife and baby's routines. With that in mind, your schedule is no longer your schedule. It will be dictated by when your wife nurses the baby, when the baby takes naps, when your wife takes naps, errands for the baby, and when you feed, change and hold the baby so it doesn't cry and scream for mom all the time. Your personal time is nonexistent.

Negotiate some of these personal items now. She's only six weeks pregnant, and you still have some clout to your relationship without the baby. Talk about mornings, evenings, and how you might handle the night schedule. Be a team player and offer to help out with feedings and watching the baby to give her a break now and then. After that's been said, mention that you'd still like to sneak in a round of golf early on a Saturday, or get in your early morning jog. At six weeks, she's not yet fully aware of how demanding a two-month old can be. Newborns do sleep quite a bit, yet they also fuss, cry, scream, spit-up, poop, cry more, scream, make all sorts of messes all over you, and fuss all day long too. It will drive you both insane. If you don't work in some of these personal-time events now, you'll never get them back. She'll say something like; "You want to go play golf for five hours? Must be nice to leave the house and have half a day to yourself – no screaming, poop, or bouncing around for two hours trying to get this bundle of joy to go to sleep!"

As you can see, even if you get the green light to go, you'll feel guilty as hell about it. And she'll make you pay for it that night. She'll make it pretty obvious that she's not getting up all night to nurse, feed, or burp the baby back to sleep. It will go something like this: "Honey, I made a couple of extra bottles for the baby down in the fridge. I also put out some clean burp cloths, diapers, and wipes in the nursery. Goodnight, love you." You're toast. That lovely little bundle of joy is yours all night!

It's 1:00 a.m. and I wake to a screaming baby, get up, feed, burp, and put her back down to sleep. It's 2 a.m., and more screaming again. I look over at my wife, who doesn't budge. She's asleep or pretending to be asleep, waiting for my ass to get out of bed and tend to our little one. I get up; the poopy diaper has leaked and is all over baby's clothes and bedding. My first instinct is to go get my wife. As I walk back down the hall to rouse her, I remember that she's played me. She gave me golf, now she's taking away my nights sleep.

Back to the nursery, baby still screaming, I take off the runny poop diaper, clean, wipe, re-wipe, and change the baby's clothes. Next, I pull off the crib or bassinette's sheets that have been splattered with wet, smelly urine. I search the nursery for new sheets, baby still screaming, and can't find any. After turning on all the lights in the room, I'm now totally awake and find the sheets. After changing, I rock baby, bounce, cuddle, and attempt to soothe her back to sleep. Forty-five minutes later and she's asleep, and I lay her back down and quietly walk back to my bedroom.

Now its 4 a.m., baby's screaming again! I'm barely back to sleep, so I nudge my wife, hoping to get some relief. She doesn't move. I don't move either. She waits me out for two minutes and still hasn't moved. Baby is still screaming. "Don't worry, I'll get up again!" I say. I roll out of bed, realizing it's feeding time. I stumble down the stairs to the kitchen, grab a bottle, trip going back up the stairs, and stagger like a zombie down the hall to the nursery. After picking her up, I stick a bottle's soft tip in her mouth and she instantly quiets down.

As I sit in the dark room, baby in my arms, I embrace the silence. My beautiful little baby girl, warm against my arms, sips away at her bottle. "I love you," I whisper to her as she nurses away at her supply of milk. All of the screaming, crying, and pooping of the night thus far, fades away. This is my little girl. I will sacrifice many things in life for her benefit, as that's what being a parent is about. Sleep depravation will be easy compared to what's ahead. Think about when she's 16 and wants to borrow the car...holy shit!

It's now 4:30 in the morning, baby is fed and back to sleep, and I'm already thinking about having to rise up in two hours to get ready for work. I fall into bed, steal some covers from my sympathetic wife, and try to get to sleep. It's now 5 a.m. and the clock is staring at me as if saying – go to sleep you dumb ass. I finally doze off only to wake up an hour later to my wife hacking up a lung in the bathroom...hhhhhaaaaaackkkkkk! Morning sickness – it's my new alarm clock.

I'd like to say that this is an instance of an isolated night, but it's not. Even if you're not feeding, changing, or burping baby all night long, your wife will wake you up anyway. Again, your pain is her pain...you're a team, remember!

Preggo-Stat temperature: HIGH

A sudden spike in hormone levels results in erratic behavior not seen before. Avoid any long conversations with her, which could lead to you saying something stupid. Non-medically dangerous spotting, or bleeding after urinating, can happen at this point, yet have her call the doctor so she can have it checked.

Week 7

What's Up Doc?

Today is our first appointment with the doctor. We learn that our doctor is wonderful. She has a way with words that calms the anxiety and unknown events that pregnancy may bring. She also has a way with running about 30 minutes behind on her patient schedule.

Her waiting room is stocked with the latest parenting magazines, books, and brochures. As I thumb through the latest mag, I notice that most are full of helpful tips for new parents and preparing for baby. Most of the guides and magazines are aimed more towards the mom, yet many seem to target dads too. The father's role has definitely changed since my dad was a new parent back in the 70's. Dads were not allowed in the birthing room, and at that time held more of a provider role for the family. Dads woke up in the morning with very little involvement with the baby, went to work, and came home to dinner on the table, read the newspaper, held the baby for a short while, and then finished up with any household man chores that needed to be done.

But these magazines had vivid pictures of the dad changing diapers, bottle-feeding, and taking the baby for a walk in the stroller. There was even an ad with a picture of a baby carrier that goes around the chest and holds the baby, which portrayed three dads with babies in these carriers hanging out at a baseball game together! Where are the Moms in all of these pictures? I'll tell you where they are – they're at home taking naps, or at a girl's night out with other new moms doing sake bombs. They need a break from breast feeding, crying, fussing, and tending to a baby all day. Yes, being a new mom is stressful. And being a new bad is also stressful. Both of you will need a break from baby now and then.

Yet, today's new dads have more responsibilities than our fathers had. Dads today are expected to carry around diaper bags at the mall, while wearing babies strapped to their chest. They're expected to know how to mix a bottle of formula, what diaper cream to apply to the baby's butt and what stage of diapers to buy at the store. Dads today are expected to be moms…minus the boobs and breast-feeding part. The parenting roles have come together in terms of taking care of a baby. Yes, the male is still a provider, the hunter and gatherer of the old fatherhood, yet the wife may be a provider too. The role of the sexes continues to evolve and nurturing a newborn is just another example of this change. Step up, it's time to embrace daddy-hood for all it has become; otherwise you'll just be a worthless piece of meat that your wife complains about to her girlfriends on girl's night out.

Don't get me wrong; I wanted to be more involved as a new dad. I couldn't wait to hold that little baby in my arms, and really didn't care if I would be changing dirty diapers. In fact, I am proud of some of the material that comes out of our little guy. "Hey honey, it's green this time." Your role will reach new levels in your marriage and one must prepare for these expectations. You might have some questions at this first visit with the doctor, but for the most part you'll be told to be supportive, loving, and helpful over the next nine months. Your wife may have a long list of questions; so let her ask them all. She needs reassurance from the doctor that she can ask anything at these appointments. You need to just sit there, hold her hand, and talk about all of the great things you can't wait to do with your new little one. You've done your part. You stuck your penis in her and one of your little swimmers managed to fertilize one of her eggs. Be happy and go back to being her man slave.

Preggo-Stat temperature: MEDIUM

Her mood could go from low to high if she doesn't like her doctor. Proceed with caution. Her uterus has doubled in size, which puts additional pressure on her bladder. She'll be making more trips to the bathroom, and morning sickness may be in full swing. You should also make a list of questions to ask her doctor at some point during her first appointment.

Week 8

Books

The next stop for most new preggo suburbanites on the way home from their first doctor appointment is the book store. Now that it's a bit more official, my wife found the need to stock up on nine years of reading material and cram it into nine months.

You'll probably run into other pregnant couples in the baby aisle, and smile politely at them. You'll have small talk and ask questions like, "When are you due?" "Is this your first?" "Where are you going to deliver?" Questions that you'll want to ask but won't are, "Are you freaking out as much as I am?" Or to the husband, "I wonder how the hell this thing is going to come out of my wife's vagina?" Or "Are you afraid that you're going to poke the baby's head when you have sex with your wife?" Either way, you'll both politely compliment one another and then go cry in the self-help section on the way out.

You're now in a special circle of trust – a circle of pregnant people who have many questions but act like they have it all figured out. This is supplemented with the knowledge that one gets from buying 28 pregnancy books and reading them cover-to-cover over the next 28 weeks.

You'll read books that cover topics such as, "What's going on in your uterus this week." You'll learn new terms like neural tube, placenta, umbilical cord and after-birth. You'll see pictures, diagrams, and videos that you'll want to look away from, yet find yourself still gawking at because that's all going to come out of your wife. You'll start to wonder if you'll ever look between your wife's legs again. You'll keep reading and reading until you run into another preggo couple that you can exchange all of your newfound knowledge with.

Next time you see your other preggo friends, you'll be armed with random facts, stories, and knowledge about pregnancy. It will be a dual of sorts and at times it may sound a bit like *Jeopardy*.

- I'll take Week 14 for $1000 Alex.

- What fluid is released from your baby's body which then absorbs into the amniotic fluid around him?

- What is urine?

Yes! That is correct. Your baby can now pee, as well as squint and possibly suck his thumb. Cool – sounds kind of like your college days…drink, pee in the front yard, pass out and fall asleep in it, and wake up nursing a hangover.

This kind of detailed knowledge will lead to long conversations with other preggo couples at dinner parties. Now that you're in this new circle of friends, you'll find that it's a bit like a nine-month book club at times. You might run into some other preggo friends at a specialty baby store and say, "What week are you guys in? Oh, week 19…did you know that your baby should be able to hear your voice now? Yeah, no kidding." You'll watch as your buddy gets down and starts talking to his wife's belly right there in the store. "Hey little dude, this is your dad talking to you…now go to your room!" You'll share a good laugh together, buy some over priced onesies that your precious baby will spit up and dump all over, go get a decaf mocha-chino, and drive back to your home with more books in hand.

After you've had your first child, you will never read these books again. They'll collect dust in some cabinet or be given to the next preggo couple that you'll pass the torch to. Then you'll have no books, and feel the need to go out and buy updated versions of previous books or new pregnancy books. Pregnancy to a man is nothing like that to a woman. We are mere spectators. You don't know squat about being pregnant, so read your ass off and be that alpha male that can rattle off random baby knowledge. This will up you're your status as a soon-to-be dad in your new crowd of preggo friends.

Preggo-Stat temperature: LOW

The excitement of the official news from her doctor should trump any increase in hormone levels. Her breasts may be growing, as they prepare for lactation. Nausea and vomiting may continue, and she might have a harder time getting comfortable for a good night's sleep. As you think of other questions to ask your doctor, write them down in a journal that the both of you can access over the course of the pregnancy.

Week 9

I'm So Sick and Tired

My wife continues to have bad morning sickness. Some women have it worse than others, and mine is one of them. The evenings are tough too. Even when she squeezes in a nap, the after dinner hours can be uncomfortable for her. The odd part about the recent weeks is that these sick phases tend to disappear when we've got something fun lined up for the weekend.

We had a one week vacation planned from months earlier, as well as a couple of long weekend trips lined up in Las Vegas and Mexico. Somehow when these events arrived, her moaning and tiredness were gone. She had no problem hanging out at the pool all day long in Mexico. She went sightseeing, shopping, and was quite pleasant to be with. The following month in Las Vegas, she hit the tables, ate out at expensive restaurants, and walked around the strip without complaining about her feet hurting. Amazing!

Then when we returned home, the symptoms came back. I'm tired, I can't make dinner, I need a pillow, my stomach hurts, I just puked this morning and I need a nap. There was more. It was incredible! This was another one of those rights of passage in pregnancy. Don't question it, but do remember not to try and call her on it. You'll be wrong, so what's the point? As well as being wrong, you'll dig yourself into a hole and have to find a way to dig your pitiful behind out of it. Don't back track - the goal is survival. You'll never be right, so quit trying to call her bluff.

She'll be ready to play on game day, but may call in sick during practice all week long. I think we all remember someone like this in our childhood days. I had a soccer teammate that always seemed to get hurt during practice. He'd sit on the sidelines while the rest of us ran our asses off all week long. Then game day came around and he was ready to play. Seeing that he was an excellent player, our coach usually let him play as we could count on him for a goal or two. I saw the same scenario with other kids in basketball, football, and even a brief stint in marching band in Jr. High. What's with these kinds of people? How the hell can you think you're that much better than me that you can sit around on your lazy butt all week long while bitching about a sore toe or bruised leg, and then miraculously heal and be 100% on game-day? Well, now I get it, because I'm married to it!

The temporary relief that will get you through this first 12 weeks is fostered by the realization that you might actually get to have sex again in the 2nd trimester. And if you're lucky, it will be plentiful. More on that later, yet I feel that it's quite relevant to mention it now, since you'll be walking through a field of emotional preggo land mines during the first three months.

Preggo-Stat temperature: HIGH

Run for cover, you're under attack! Your wife may or may not be showing; yet she feels very pregnant. Take evening walks after dinner together. Mood swings become more predominant, unfortunately it's perfectly normal.

Week 10

Name Game

Now that you have your books, at least three of them will be dedicated to just names. With the Internet now, it seems odd that one would pay 20 bucks a pop for a book that is basically a spreadsheet of names. There are no baby stories and no mention of pregnancy terms or facts about the nine months to follow. It's just a book filled with names, A – Z. Even though your wife already has the names pre-selected in her head for all of your soon-to-be kids, she'll find the need to torture you with possible other selections.

She selected these names long before she met you. These names date back to her teen years, and are related to some TV show she watched, book she read, or boyfriend she had at the time. She has already "called" these names to her close girlfriends, so that they cannot claim them for their babies. She may have changed the spelling a bit, or maybe altered the shortened version of the name, yet it's a done deal. You can throw your selected names in the hat, but they have no chance. Maybe she'll throw you a bone on naming the middle name, but that's about all the input you'll get.

Our first child was a girl, which she named Sophia. I had absolutely no chance on naming her. My wife had called that one out long ago, even down to the spelling. Our second child was a boy. I really liked the name Drew for a boy. I was vetoed with the name Jack.

Our third child was a boy as well. I really liked the name Tyler (I still liked the name Drew, yet my wife told me that it could not be used now because this was a name which still gives some reference to our second child – even though his name is Jack). That makes absolutely no sense, but I'm married to a crazy, emotional, pregnant wife that gets to make up the rules. I did eventually get the name Tyler, as our third child was a boy. Lucky for me, my wife agreed with me early in her pregnancy that she did like the name Tyler and it could be a contender.

Even though I am claiming this victory, she attempted to trump the name until her eighth month. She bought different baby books, bounced names off of friends and relatives, all along knowing that Tyler would more than likely be the name. She would still attempt to wear the crown and take me down in the final bout of naming our third child. If she could find another name that would somehow bring additional meaning to our child, she could then take me down with an unsuspecting right hook and knock my name out.

In the end, she slapped the seal of approval on the name Tyler. By giving her sign off on the name, she attempted to make it look like she chose the name and had the final say. What the hell is this about? I already need approval to take a crap, as I'm taking all of five minutes to myself while the baby screams and the other kids drive her up the wall. How dare I think that I can just walk into the bathroom, close the door for privacy, and take a dump in peace and quiet? No – I should do personal stuff like that after the kids have gone to bed. I should be helping her out and giving her breaks for naps, instead of taking trips to the commode in the middle of the day! I'm exaggerating a bit, but your wife will constantly be looking at ways to get some rest and will tear you down if she doesn't get to do so. Taking a trip to the toilet will no longer give you any privacy once you have kids anyway. My three-year old is amazed with poop. If he knows or hears of someone that is about to have a bowel movement, he wants to come and watch. He wants to know what color it is, big or small, long or short, and if it hurt or not pushing it out. Some of the best bonding time I had with my son occurred while I was in the throes of a major pooper.

As for the name, I reclaimed Tyler as "my" name and made sure to let everyone around me know that Tyler was my glory. I held my ground on that name from day one and beat her down in time. Tyler was my victory. I had to take her twelve rounds, yet I got the TKO! She took care of the middle name this time though, but it's hardly bragging rights compared to the first!

Preggo-Stat temperature: MEDIUM

Keep her calm by actually listening to her when she talks. I know it is hard, but you can do it. Her clothes may start to be a bit tight as her belly grows. Be sensitive to her weight gain, as she may need to take a trip to the mall for maternity clothes. She might complain about being hungry, yet certain foods that she used to like will make her feel nauseous. Crackers make a great snack, so pick up some of her favorites at the grocery.

Week 11

Secret Code of Sharing the News

My wife woke up this morning and said it's time to start telling people that we're pregnant. Her 12-week doctor appointment is later this week, and if doc says all looks well, we'll starting sharing the news.

The main reason she brought this up was to clarify the order of this process. There is a very strict code set by women on how this works. I had no clue. I thought we'd just start telling people. Oh no. I couldn't be more wrong. My wife states, "You can't just tell people. There are rules so that everyone hears the news from us without hearing it from someone else." I reply, "Of course. I knew that – I was just testing you." I really had no idea about this strict code, but then again, I don't really know zilch about being pregnant.

As she began to blab aloud about everyone we had to tell, I decided to just follow her lead on this one. First, the parents must be told. They should be told in a special way, or maybe in some kind of surprise fashion. My parents lived out of state, so we decided to send them a pair of small booties with a note inside to call us when they received it. It was a fun way to share the news, and it definitely brought tears to my parents' eyes. My mom and dad were ready for grandchildren, as it would be the first on my side of the family. My wife's parents were local, so we visited them in person to share the news. We brought them a gift as well to enable harvesting the surprise factor.

Next to be told were our brothers and sisters, all of who were asked not to tell any other extended family member until we'd had a chance to do so first. Again, we're attempting to tell everyone we need to before the news leaks out and my wife has to field the phone call, "How come you didn't tell me you were pregnant?" This would violate the code, and the mission would be a failure.

After that we met some of our close friends for lunch to share the news. Again, we asked them not to tell any other mutual friends in order to preserve the code. Well, that didn't happen. The news leaked out. And it wasn't from a friend, it was me!

While I was outside later that day, my neighbor stopped me to chat in the driveway. As we were talking, he suddenly shifted topics and asked, "Hey, what's new in your world?" I replied, "I'm going to be a dad!" Oh damn, I am breaking the code. I quickly told him not to say anything, as some of our neighbors were mutual friends. "Awesome. I won't say anything," he said. Well, that really meant that he wouldn't say anything except to his wife. Then his wife will share the news inadvertently with someone, and the next thing you know, the whole block will know, and our friends will be calling my wife saying, "How come you didn't tell me you were pregnant?"

Well, that's what happened. Within an hour, the phone was ringing and my wife was fielding the phone call. I had broken command, and the control tower was being attacked. She quickly covered with a reply, "Yes, I was going to call you today. I don't know how the news got out." I had to say something. I couldn't let her ship sink. "I leaked the news honey. I am the mole." While I waited for a crazy, pregnant wife's emotional breakdown, instead she replied, "Thank you." Even though the code was broken, she didn't break it. She had an out and the mission could go on.

That evening, we made phone calls to other friends, aunts and uncles, cousins, and any other family members that we thought we should call. After the four-hour phone-a-thon, we followed up with an E-mail blast to everyone. This would cover any other leaks and bring the announcement full circle. Yes, we did it. Protocol was broken, yet the commander considered the mission uncompromised.

Preggo-Stat temperature: MEDIUM

Be aware of intra-day mood swings. New symptoms of constipation or heartburn may coincide with her food likes and dislikes. Morning sickness may continue into the evening.

Week 12

Throwing up Everywhere

Is the morning sickness ever going to stop? I have had the unfortunate realization that my wife will be hacking up stomach fluid, saliva, and God only knows what else for at least another four months. For many pregnant women, the morning sickness stops after about 12 weeks. For my wife, she seems to carry some evil pregnancy tapeworm in her body that doesn't want to give up.

At 5 a.m., she hawks up another loogie of stomach spit, drawing it all of the way up her throat and into her mouth. Out it comes into the sink with a trace of drool hanging down from her lips, dangling and waiting for another hack to release it. I no longer need an alarm clock, as she has become the morning bell that will wake me for months to come.

As I get out of bed, walk to the bathroom where she stands over the sink, I rub her back hoping to comfort her and identify with the harsh pains that women take on during pregnancy. Her hair hangs down around her face, and she looks up to see my reflection in the mirror. I smile at her and say, "Its okay honey." She looks at me with drool hanging from her mouth, a few strands of hair stuck to her lips, and a flush face from hacking out hairballs the last five minutes. She says, "Hand me a towel…in fact, hand me your towel." Well, at least she still has her sense of humor! I get her a towel, and she wipes away the spit from around her mouth. She is a beautiful sight – a pure beam of morning pregnancy. Wait, she's not done. The towel drops on the floor and she's back at it over the sink. I run for cover and head for the toilet to hide (you'll soon find that even the toilet will no longer be a place of privacy). She turns on the sink to wash down the last hack-fest, and walks over to get a towel. This time it's my towel. After she's done wiping off the drool, she looks up at me and smiles!

You always get to share in the torture in some shape or form. Indirectly, you will be going through the same things as your partner. In a way, that's what pregnancy for a guy is all about. In good times and in bad times, in sickness and in health, you're in it together. At least for now, it's coming out of her mouth…you still have pregnancy gas to look forward to!

Preggo-Stat temperature: HIGH

She's tired, puking her guts out in the morning and afterwards picky about her food. Hide in the garage! Heartburn or acid indigestion will continue as her uterus gets larger and pushes against her stomach. Talk to your doctor about safe ways to treat this discomfort, as it will probably continue throughout her pregnancy. All of it!

Week 13

My Own Personal Taxi Driver

I would hope by now that you have come to the conclusion that you have a unique situation for nine months. For every wedding you go to, for every dinner party you attend, and for every date night, evening dinner, afternoon tailgate party, and any other event that might have an open bar or offer alcohol, you have a designated driver. Yes, you have a DD for nine months! I am not advocating drinking, yet you have to admit that this will be awesome. There's nothing more fun that a bitchy, achy, whiny pregnant wife would like to do nothing more than drive your plastered ass home for the next 38 weeks. What a privilege. She is going to love you even more. In fact, now you can both hack, yak and throw-up together in the morning. You can both have headaches and puke your guts out. You can both walk around the house in your pajamas the next day until 4 o'clock in the afternoon. The only thing you need to remember is, don't lead with it when you go out. By the third or forth time, it will be a given, but you don't want to throw this special perk in her face. She'll make you pay for it later.

When the invitation comes in the mail for a wedding next month or a dinner party next weekend, play it cool. Act just as you did before. "Honey, did you see that invitation to the Dicksucker's wedding, whoever that is? Oh, she was an old college friend of yours. Should I put it down on the calendar for us to attend? Yes, ok, I'll write it down."

Follow normal protocol and she'll never expect what's going on in your sick little mind. Yes, I can get wasted that night! I wonder if it will be a full bar or just beer and wine. Or maybe it will be an open bar, and they will have top shelf liquor. Yeah, that's awesome. I can get lit and feel guilt free! Sure, she might be pissed off once she figures out how your little plan works, but what is she going to do about it? Not go? It's her friend's wedding. She has to go. This is her moment to show all of the other non-pregnant, non-married, no kid having bitches that she's knocked up and having a baby. She's going to be a mom and you're not...that's the cat-peeing territorial message that she needs to send out to all of the other wannabe mommies at the wedding. Sure, the bride is the center of attention, but I'd argue that a pregnant woman would be next in line on center stage.

Everybody likes pregnant women. They secrete a fragrance that attracts happiness. Women eat that stuff up. They love talking about being a mom because they've grown up playing dolls and playing mommy. It's subconsciously built into their DNA and women adore pregnancy. Especially at a wedding, as that will be the order of events in life. When are you going to get married? Now that you're married, when are you going to have kids? Oh, you have a baby girl, when are you going to have another baby? And it goes on and on until you march your ass down to the doctor and get sterilized. Yes, your wife will order you to get a vasectomy at some point in your life if you want to have sex again. She'll have gone through enough diapers with goop oozing from the sides and you'll come home one day to, "I can't do this any longer. If you want to ever have sex again, go make your appointment. Otherwise, don't touch me!"

I got a bit off subject there, so back to the DD strategy. Go about your business as usual, drive to the wedding, and offer to get her some kind of non-alcoholic drink when you go to get your double Jack and Coke. I learned from a friend of mine to always make it a double at weddings. Those lines at the bar can get long, and you never know when they are going to shut them down. She might ask what you're having (or she may be able to smell it if you go with the double strategy), so follow with something like, "Well, at least one of us can drink." Yes, she's on your side, well not completely. For one or two drinks she won't really notice, but after that she'll realize that you're getting wasted. She'll start by saying under her breath, "Why is he out break dancing with a drink in his hand? I've never seen him do the conga line before. What's up with him getting shit faced while I'm pregnant--and how is he going to drive home?" Then it will hit her. "I'm driving his drunk-behind home." From that moment on, she'll know what to expect at any future event, so make your first one count.

If you're lucky, she'll laugh at your sad impression of the robot dance, have a great time giving off her scent of pregnancy to all of the sorry wannabe non-pregnant women, and drive you home. If you really scored on the wife scale, she'll take you through the late night drive-through at Mc Burger Bell and let you yell your order across the seat at the loudspeaker: "I'll take a number 4 with a Jack and Coke..." When you arrive at your driveway, whiz in the bushes, walk in the house, and pass out in your clothes, she'll be thinking about the hell you're going to feel in the morning. That alone will make her feel a little bit better about her nine months of sobriety.

Preggo-Stat temperature: MEDIUM

Friends, family, and co-workers are full of advice, which could lead to evening mood swings. Answer any of these questions or statements with, "Well honey, let's look in the pregnancy book and see what it says. That should help." Her second trimester has begun, and she may begin to feel less nauseous than before. She may feel more energetic and her sex drive might be heightened during this trimester.

Week 14

Horny

I've been waiting for it, and it finally came. Day three, week fourteen, the horny stage of the second trimester has begun. I came home for a "nooner" and it was the best ten minutes I've had in a while. Yes, it was planned. We had talked about it the night before and stayed up too late watching HGTV, so we postponed it until the next day while our two kids would be in pre-school.

I came home for lunch and started with a boob sandwich. I followed that up with some quick foreplay, and took her down to the bedroom floor and earned some quick rug burns. She pushed me off, flipped me on my back, and rode me like a horse without a saddle. Her breasts were bigger and her nipples were ten times more sensitive than before. She screamed for more, as she went into one of the longest orgasms she's had in a while. This pregnancy sex is awesome! Sweat dripping down her body, I ran my hands up and down her back and stroked her hair. She leaned over my chest and I grabbed her and rolled her back over, as we went into another position. Wow – we're going on ten minutes here…this might be a new record for what was supposed to be a quickie. She grabs onto a pillow, moans for more, and I spank her bottom just before I can't last any longer. Yes!

Pregnancy sex is awesome. I was patient and the libido had emerged again for both of us. I've been told that the spark may come and go over this term, and that certain positions may not work like they used to as her belly gets bigger. In either case, enjoy exploring every inch of your wife's pregnant body. Her senses are heightened which can lead to some fresh discoveries on her new curves. Take pleasure in it while you can, as you'll be in the sex desert for a few months after the baby comes. The drought will eventually end, yet it will be a long walk to the oasis of doin' it.

Preggo-Stat temperature: LOW

Her belly may be showing more, giving evidence of "baby on board." Her appetite may start to escalate, since she's eating for two.

Spoil her with some of her favorite meals, and make a late night run for her pregnancy food cravings…and have more sex!

Week 15

Mind Reader

M y wife seems to think that I have ESP lately. I came home from work with her asking, "Why didn't you pick up dinner? Why didn't you pick up milk at the grocery? I thought you were going to pick up a gift for the party tomorrow?" Huh? I don't remember having these discussions. Was I asleep when you told me this? Was I not in the room? Did I miss some honey to-do list you left me on the kitchen counter? What the F. I don't know what the hell you're talking about!

Yesterday I came home from the office, threw on some shorts and a tee shirt, popped open a brewski, and started to get dinner ready before my lovely bride got home. I had marinated some steaks from the night before, grabbed some corn on the cob, and headed outside to light the BBQ. As I lit all three burners on the grill, I sat and thought about how happy my wife would be to find me preparing dinner before she got home. She would say, "Oh honey, how nice of you to get dinner on the table tonight. That's one last thing for me to worry about. I love you so much honey!" I smiled knowing that I was being a good husband. I even thought it might help build up some points that I could cash in later for a guy's night out or a round of golf, and both guilt free.

Well, that's not quite what happened. She came home just as I was setting the table and about to take the steaks from the grill. The corn was ready, and I had made a salad too. "Hi honey," she said. "I hope you remembered that I'm not eating meat anymore with this pregnancy. It makes my stomach turn." With my grilling tongs in hand, I said, "I don't remember that. I thought you said that you can't eat cheeseburgers anymore." She goes onto say, "Uh no. I said all red meat. Weren't you listening? I'll puke if I do."

I ran to the fridge, pulled out some chicken breasts, and quickly threw a couple on the grill. From down the hall she asks, "Did you pick up the eggs I needed to make a cake tonight for Jack's birthday party this weekend?" I don't remember anything about eggs. There was no discussion of eggs for me to pick up. "I forgot to pick them up honey. I'll run down to the grocery right after dinner." I thought that would be a sufficient cover.

As the chicken began to sear on the grill, I cut it open with a knife so the flames could cook the insides. Still dumbfounded by the red meat comment, I pulled the steaks off of the grill, turned up the heat, and closed the cover over the chicken breasts. I went back inside the house to get some BBQ sauce. She's sitting at the kitchen island, yapping away about how bad her day was and how tired she is…the usual first 30 minutes of any conversation when I get home from the office. She states, "My back hurts so bad that it makes my hips hurt, which makes my feet hurt. I really need to try and take a nap once a day. The kids drove me crazy today, so I couldn't lie down. It must be so nice to just sit in an office all day by yourself, honey."

There it was. She slid in the, "It must be so nice" line. She uses this one regularly. It must be so nice to – add any item that she can no longer do, but you can because you're not pregnant. "It must be so nice to…have coffee, drink wine, not pee every five minutes, fit into your clothes, be comfortable at night, not have morning sickness, fit into your shoes (later on your wife's feet will swell up like water balloons), and eat cheeseburgers! There's not much you can say to this one. She's pregnant, emotional, and says whatever the hell she wants.

So far, I'm not scoring any points for dinner or the errand I missed. As I go back out to the grill to brush the BBQ sauce on her chicken, she says, "I'm really not hungry. I'm going to go lie down for a bit." No you're not, you whiny B. I just made dinner, made a second dinner to cover my first dinner, and I don't even remember these conversations to begin with! As she leaves the kitchen and heads over to the couch, I sit down and eat my steak. The kids are due home any minute from my sister's house, so I wolf down my food and get ready for the next storm. Baths, books, and bedtime – that's my next two hours, then out to the grocery to get the eggs that I supposedly forgot about.

Just as I'm done with the kid's baths, my wife comes in and says, "I'm going to make you a list so you stop forgetting to do these things for me. I really need your help right now." Help right now – your lazy ass was just napping on the couch while I'm taking care of dinner and the kids! That's helping in my book. After reading to the kids, tucking them in bed, I come back down to the kitchen. She hands me a list of items to get at the grocery. Forty-five minutes later, I'm back with the goods, eggs and all. She's started the cake and I'm ready to imprint my butt in the couch. Put a fork in me, I'm done.

Preggo-Stat temperature: HIGH

Your wife may still feel nauseous at times, yet it should not be as bad as the first trimester. She's having a harder time getting comfortable at night. Score some points and stop by the local baby store to get her a special pregnancy-sleeping pillow. It's a long, body pillow that she can tuck up and around her belly and legs for support and comfort.

Week 16

Gas

I like to make noises that come from my butt. I think it's funny. There's something so childish about it that it still makes me laugh. I mean, who doesn't appreciate a great fart joke? The woopy-cushion changed my life when I was seven years old. Placing that little pink cushion on a chair of some unsuspecting individual made me laugh just anticipating the surprise sound. Fffffffffffaaaaaaaaaaaarrrrrrrrrrrrrrrtttttttt - pure comedy in its cheapest form. Sometimes it was a long one, or short one, or action-packed bursts, or machine gun or runny patterns, it really didn't matter. It always made me laugh.

The remote control fart gag gift I received years later in life changed my life all over again. If you haven't seen it, it's a small 2" receiver with a speaker on it that you place near your victim. You then hold the mini remote control in your hand; press the button when your prey is near the 2" unit, and presto...Fart! And just like the whoopee-cushion I used with my seven-year old friends, the remote control version was just as useful around my co-workers. My assistant was the first victim. While she sat in her cube outside my office, I hid the tiny receiver in her bottom desk drawer. When she came back from her smoke break and was complaining about her boyfriend who she'd just called on her cell phone, I waited for her to get comfortable in her cube. As it got quiet, I pushed the remote button. Ffffffffffffaaaaaaaaaarrrrrttttt! She jumped and started to blush. Co-workers in cubes around her peaked over their respective cubicles. I sat quietly trying to hold back the laughter. Again, I pushed the remote control button...Ffffffffffffffaaaaaaarrttttttttt! Now she's starting to get more than a little flustered.

I look out to see what's going on. Eventually, I can't help but bust a gut and laugh my ass off. The remote control farter is a must have for any office setting.

Now my wife is practicing the art. I don't think she even knew how to break wind around me before she was pregnant. It never stopped me, as I let em' rip every night in bed as my belly settled and the gas moved through my stomach and eventually echoed under the sheets. She has experienced many of my "Dutch ovens" under the sheets, and heard the bellowing of my finest achievements from the bathroom, and somehow still finds me attractive enough to have sex with.

I find it quite humorous; yet know she at times is embarrassed about the sounds exuding from her caboose. Either way, its part of the package, and I now know that when she craves Mexican food for dinner, I had better be prepared for the evening that lies ahead of me.

My efforts smell bad, but I'm used to it. Hers are long and loud, and can linger. The smell is killing me and I think it might be killing our houseplants too. The odor is somewhere between the smell of moldy cheese, a dead skunk, and burnt rubber. The even more impressive part is its staying power. Her best work hangs on for what seems like hours and can move from room to room without losing power.

It's like she's leaving a breadcrumb trail around the house. I can follow it. She let it rip in the kitchen, then moved to the TV room, and then proceeded down the hall to the laundry room. I confronted her, or should I say complimented her on what was fast developing into a skill set. "Honey, you can really let em' rip eh? These preggo things are nasty!" She laughs but walks off a bit embarrassed. I then hear another fffffffffaaaaaaarrrrrrttttttttttt! She's at it again. I'm dying laughing at this point. She's farther down the hall by the front closet. "I can't help it," she says. "My body is just full of gas and I can't hold it in." I run for the back door while gasping for air. I think my Dutch ovens have met their match.

Preggo-Stat temperature: LOW

It may be a bit early, yet you might feel the baby kick for the first time. Ask her if she's feeling less nauseous. Rub her back and shoulders to ease any tension she might be feeling as the baby starts to move around more inside her bump.

Week 17

Where's my Dinner

The cravings are really kickin' in. It started with ice cream, then pizza, and later grilled cheese. Lately it has been pasta, specifically spaghetti. And it has to come with garlic bread. No meatballs, no fancy sauces, just good ole' spaghetti with garlic bread.

Last evening, I arrived home at about 4:30, ran upstairs, changed my clothes, ran back down and whisked the kids outside to give my lovely wife some breathing room from her crazy day. If you're reading this and you don't have kids, don't worry...your wife will still beckon you home early to soothe her in some way. It may be to start a bath for her, pick up some food, or just simply to tell you how uncomfortable she is. Maybe she'll have diarrhea and need you to get her more toilet paper because you're lazy ass forgot to put a new roll on the toilet paper holder the last time you took a dump. Whatever the sudden phone call of needing you to rush home, you'll get plenty of them before and after your beautiful baby arrives.

Anyway, as I blew bubbles outside with the kids, my wife begins to talk about spaghetti. She wants it for dinner. She's been thinking about it all day. She needs it now. Ok. Here's an idea. Let's make it. I know, this is a bit crazy, but I think even my wife of limited talents in the kitchen can manage to boil water and drop noodles in it. Making pasta falls a close second to the complexity of making toast. I, of course, make this suggestion...better yet, I offer to make the meal. She hesitates, and then answers no. She needs garlic bread with it.

I continue to play with my wonderful kids as my wife decides how we are going to maneuver this spaghetti meal so it fits within our normal dinner hour. We've kept our kids on a great schedule when it comes to the dinner hour. We all eat together at the table, follow with a snack, some play time, baths and off to bed with a couple of books. Having routines has helped our children as well as us keep some order in an often crazy household.

Tonight was one of those nights where the routine gets hit with a curve ball. My wife continues to wander through the kitchen as if she's going to make this dinner appear by magic. I peak at her from the back yard, in between blowing bubbles for the kids, only to discover she's in front of the computer searching the Internet for the closest spaghetti restaurant. "Do you think we can order spaghetti?" she yells out the back door to me. Last time I checked, you can't. Maybe you can find a delivery service that will deliver spaghetti from a restaurant, but it doesn't work like a late-night pepperoni pizza craving.

Next step, take out. Where can we get spaghetti and garlic bread as take out. She's getting closer as we yell back and forth about restaurants that we could get take out from. By now, almost an hour has gone by, and still no spaghetti and garlic bread. At this point, I could have boiled pasta, dumped some red sauce on it, and made garlic bread from scratch, but what the hell do I know?

Remember, you don't know nada about being pregnant, so don't act like you do. You will never know, even if you've been through it ten thousand times. It is her right to throw that in your face as much as possible, so keep your mouth shut and be that wonderful husband that she married you for. Maybe you'll get some more pregnancy sex if you can bite your tongue and not answer the obvious for her.

She knows you could have made this dinner for her, that she could have stopped at the grocery store, even picked up the take out order before you came home. This is the pregnancy game or dance as some may call it. She gets to torture you with questions and situations that you can't possibly answer or react to in the right way. You may think you have the most delicate, caring answer to calm her pregnancy craziness, but you don't because you don't know anything about being pregnant and never will.

I have to repeat that many times in this book in order to get this point across - shut your mouth and just listen. End of story. By now, I've offered to go pick up the take out order of spaghetti and garlic bread, and even take the kids with me so she can have a bit of additional quiet time. Good idea, but wrong answer. She's put in all of the hard work to track down this dinner--and she will go and pick it up herself.

Another half an hour goes by and she's back. Dinner is served and the craving has been conquered. The evening routine with the kids is way off schedule, but again it doesn't really matter. She's pregnant for nine months, and the routines may be altered at times to accommodate for this. All routines that you once had will be rerouted around the nine months of pregnancy. Your wife needs your love and attention more than ever. And remember, you're trying to get some more of that pregnancy sex.

Preggo-Stat temperature: HIGH

She's gassy, nauseous and indecisive. That's not a good combination! Your wife might be feeling dizzy at times and need to lie down more often. Her dreams may be more vivid than before, so ask what she's dreaming about. Talk about any fears or anxiety that might be brought about by your soon to be new addition. Keep the lines of communication open, and take time in the evenings to speak to one other or write in her pregnancy journal.

Week 18

More Food Cravings

Over this nine month timeline, your wife will eventually find one craving that will get her through the entire pregnancy. For some it's ice cream, others it's pizza...sometimes its cookies, or maybe even a late night fast food run. For my wife it became a cheese sandwich - or in this case, cheesy with a lid. The name came about from one of those delirious pregnancy moments...tired, uncomfortable, and not making a lot of sense while she's talking. This is not to be mistaken for a grilled cheese sandwich. The cheesy with a lid is simply a piece of bread with a slice of cheese on it melted in the microwave. It's quick and easy for those preggo cravings.

I tend to make sandwiches at times with only a bottom piece of bread, which I believe is called an open-face sandwich. One evening I offered to make her a cheese sandwich she was craving, and she yelled to me while I was in the kitchen, "Put a lid on it." At first, I thought she was continuing her crazy, emotional pregnancy talk and making me her man slave was just part of the nine-month process. "Put a lid on it," are you kidding me? Now I can't talk? Put a lid on it? What the hell is that about...I've chosen to keep my mouth shut for my own protection at times (insert foot in mouth is quite common in my house), but I didn't need my wife putting the verbal smack down on me now.

I'm trying to be that caring, sensitive, giving, loving husband that asks nothing in return, yet she's starting to make it a bit difficult. I made her sandwich, and delivered it to her with a nice 30-second zap in the microwave to melt the cheese over the single slice of bread. As I handed the cheesy sandwich to her, she looked up and said, "There's only one piece of bread - can you put a lid on it?"

I laughed, as I realized that this was just one of those many pregnancy language barriers that only pregnant woman can communicate. We both had a good laugh, and I redelivered the cheesy with the traditional two pieces of bread and melted cheese in the middle, which I have done so night after night after night.

Over the next nine months, you'll find your own language barriers as your emotional wife rattles off random phrases and run-on sentences that you'll have no freakin' idea what the meaning is. That's the fun of it. She's always right and you're always trying to guess what she's talking about. This may sound like marriage in general, yet the pregnancy turns it up a few notches on the crazy scale.

Preggo-Stat temperature: MEDIUM

Her appetite continues to increase and she might be picky about what she eats. She might start snoring at night or get leg cramps. If you didn't get her that pregnancy body pillow yet, go get it for her. She's probably uncomfortable on her back or stomach, and feels best when lying on her side.

Week 19

Penis or Vagina

Today is the big day! I'm meeting my wife at 3:30 for our ultrasound where we'll be able to see the development of our little one. And the big question will be answered - boy or girl? This is our 3rd time down this road, and we've been blessed with a beautiful girl and handsome little boy already, yet I'm still in complete suspense as to what the sex will be. Thinking about the appointment today still brings a sense of wonderment to what the next chapters in our life will hold.

My first thoughts are for mom and baby to be in good health. I've thought about this a bit more with the third pregnancy, as we have not had any earlier complications with the two previous pregnancies.

With the third, you often feel like you're testing fate a bit. Thinking back to the first pregnancy and that initial ultrasound gets my heart racing again with the excitement of seeing our little baby up on the big screen (or 12" black and white monitor in this case). What an exhilarating experience it is to view your little one for the first time.

I remember seeing this little creature curled up, crossing and uncrossing her legs, turning her head and looking at us, and seeing her little profile as she gave us some great glimpses of what was yet to come. I pictured holding her for the first time, still curled up but in a blanket in my arms. All of these thoughts came back as I waited for this workday to pass by so I could get over to the doctors office. This has got to be one of the most exciting days that a soon to be dad can have.

After this appointment you may already have a name chosen and be able to call the baby by name, if you decide to find out what the sex is. We will be asking the technician to tell us. We want to know ahead of time, and so does our 5 1/2 year old daughter. She really wants a baby sister, yet said she'll be happy with another brother too. After a couple of conference calls, answering around 30 emails, and a long lunch with a client, it's nearly 3 p.m. I happily log off of my computer and head out to the elevator and down to my car. My wife calls to tell me that the appointment is not at the doctor's office, but at the radiology center at the hospital. What! I'm already at the doctor's office waiting outside the building for you. Why would you wait until 3:20 to call and tell me this? I had actually made an effort to be early for this appointment, unlike many that I walk into five or ten minutes late.

I should have remembered this from the last time we did this, but I didn't. I was in a trance - I was so eager to get to this appointment that it didn't even dawn on me that this was the one at the hospital. I zipped down the street, parked again, and managed to make it just on time. Our appointment was on a Monday afternoon and it didn't appear to be very busy. Within five minutes we were in the room and the technician was about to begin. I put my hand on my wife and could tell that she was just as excited as I was.

The technician went through all of the measurements, stopping, then typing something, starting again, stopping, taking another measurement, starting again, while at the same time walking us through what we were seeing on the big 12" monitor. We could see the head, the spine, feet, hands, legs, fingers, toes and the cute little profile of our little guy or girl. So far, so good. I was anxious, yet calm now that I could see what has been happening over the last 19 weeks. My wife was giddy, yet holding back a few tears of joy as she looked at me and felt so right in the world at this moment.

Everything felt so good. Boy or girl, it didn't matter. I am a dad, and there's nothing better in the world than being a dad. And then the money shot came on - one leg, two legs, three legs...? Yep, it was a boy! Cool! I was so excited. I love it! A boy. Wow! This is awesome. A little boy. I can't wait to hold him in my arms, and through those thin hospital blankets feel his warm little body against my chest. Boy, girl, twins, triplets, whatever God may bring you, it's a blessing. This is a special day and now it's time to get on the phone and share the news with family.

Preggo-Stat temperature: LOW

When you go in for your ultrasound (you may have gone in already), ask the doctor or assistant to print off a few additional photos of the baby for friends and family. If you're going to need childcare for your baby, start your search soon as you may need to reserve a spot for your child.

Week 20

Good-Bye Home Office

Now that we know it's a boy, the time has come to really start thinking about the room. I'd like to think that I have some say in it, seeing that it's a boy, right? Not quite. I was thinking a nice baseball theme might be nice this time. Or maybe a multi-colored blue stripe with skateboards, surfboards or perhaps a car theme. My wife entertained those thoughts with the utmost care, and then quickly re-routed my choices into much more of a whimsical theme. At first, she came to me with a blue and white room with a mural of soft, white clouds, rainbows, and little forest animals like Bambi and such in the background. Man, this is not looking good. This is not what I had in mind. I want a linebacker, not a ballet dancer.

We compromised on some kind of zoo-animal theme. Compromising in marriage, as you know means agreeing with your wife. I did manage to narrow it down a bit more to monkeys...kind of like that book about ten little monkeys jumping on the bed idea.

Our oldest child, Sophia, had a butterfly-princess theme, which has now transformed into pink, pink, and more pink, as she's grown older. Our son, Jack, has a trains, cars and planes theme. So our new little guy will have something different. That was another important objective to cover while making the decision - each room had to be unique.

Why would you re-use some of the old decorations in a new room? To a woman, that just doesn't make any sense. I have been able to reuse the crib and changing table over and over with each new child. Remember that while you're shopping for bedroom furniture for baby. Not that you'll really have much of a say in the matter, but you may be able to subliminally direct your wife towards something in a basic wood color or traditional frame that could be used for a boy or a girl.

Preggo-Stat temperature: MEDIUM

The realization that she's half way through pregnancy leaves her with bittersweet emotions. Sign up for childbirth classes at your hospital and get ready to watch one of those classic childbirth videos! Talk to her about who's going to be in the room when she gives birth and how graphic she wants her video documentary to be.

Week 21

Complications

We received a call from our doctor today that my wife has Placenta Previa. We had no idea what it was, as we've had no complications on our first two pregnancies. Previa is when the placenta begins to attach itself a bit lower than normal. Usually, the placenta, which for quick review purposes is the bag that stores the baby's nutrients, attaches itself on the side of the womb. With Previa, it begins to attach a bit lower by the cervix, which can cause more pressure to be placed on the placenta. If it continues, the woman must often be placed in a continual state of bed rest to avoid damaging the placenta, seeing that it essentially holds the baby's food supply. She would then need to have a c-section because the doctor does not want the placenta to come out before the baby. Let me elaborate, and you can picture all of this happening as you gaze at your wife's vagina while she's spread eagle in the delivery chair.

The order of delivery is baby, umbilical cord, and then placenta and afterbirth. When the placenta is lower in the womb, it would be blocking the path of the baby, and come out first. Not good. The food supply would then be cut off from the baby, which could be dangerous. Ninety percent of the time, Previa corrects itself. As your wife gets bigger, the placenta is usually pushed up into its proper place. So at this stage, we're supposed to remain positive, as it should correct by our next appointment. In the meantime, our doctor asked that she take it easy, no lifting, reduce her exercise level a bit, and are you ready for this...no sex. Yes, I'm willing to sacrifice anything for my newborn baby and wife, yet no sex?

Remember a few chapters back when I talked about how good pregnancy sex can be? It can be some of the best sex you've ever had. And now, the dream has been postponed for a bit. I'm trying to be sensitive here, yet no sex. That sucks. Even my wife agrees with me. She was ready to do it tonight. I did mention that she could still give me the "other option"...if you've been married awhile you can image how big of a laugh that got. It wasn't my birthday, she said. Yes, that's my birthday deal. If you don't have a birthday deal, get one. That's a completely different subject, but you get where I'm going with it.

So for now, we must hope that the Previa corrects on its own and try not to worry about it. The most important thing is that my wife and baby are safe and that we're as cautious as we need to be to make sure both are well taken care of. No more trips to Costco lifting 2 crates of 96 bottles of water into the cart. No more extensive walks or stroller strides for a bit. No more packing our two and a half year old around on her hip. She needs to slow down, which means I need to speed up...funny how this nine months works out.

Preggo-Stat temperature: MEDIUM

Any complications along the way can lead to all kinds of mood swings. Talk with your doctor if you need additional advice on how to communicate with your wife about these issues in pregnancy.

Week 22

Quiet Before the Storm

Today I got home around 4:30, expecting two kids to come running out to the garage screaming, "Dad, dad, dad!" Instead, complete silence. The kids are nowhere to be seen and my beautiful pregnant wife is not in the kitchen preparing my five-course dinner...yes, that was a joke. It's rare that I come home to a quiet home. It's usually filled with plenty of noise from my five-year-old girl and my two-year-old boy.

Quite often I walk in the garage door to Spiderman and Cinderella or batman and tinker bell. My son may be running through the house belting out his best train noises, and my daughter may be flying around the house as a fairy or ballerina princess. Sometimes it's a small garage band made up of keyboards and drums that fills the house. After a long day of work, I'm always eager to see their smiling faces and get a big welcome home hug.

But today, there was none of that. It was a noise that I have come to cherish - absolute silence. Amazing. You'll come to look forward to this just as much as being with your new bundle of joy. There's nothing like a baby screaming for two hours straight as you try to feed, change, and rock the child back to sleep. I believe many new parents have called this quiet time, the new happy hour for parents.

Your free time on the weekends is now crammed with mowing the lawn, cleaning the garage, picking up the house, and finishing all of your other house projects. While you may have done that before, now you must do it during your few free hours of the weekend. A baby changes everything.

I would encourage all the new dads out there to keep some of house projects to a minimum if you can for a few months after the baby is born. You're going to be extremely tired from your wife waking you up every time she's feeding the baby, changing the baby in the middle of the night, or rocking the baby back to sleep. More than likely, in some shape or form you'll be taking care of the baby just as much as your wife. Even if you decide to take turns nightly, or within the night, it all leads to tired parents. Your wife will feel like she's nothing but a milk machine and you'll feel like you're her newly hired assistant.

Eventually, she'll burn out from lack of sleep, blow up on you when you get home from work, and then you're really screwed. You'll feel guilty for not being able to live up to her baby-nurturing expectations, and she'll feel so exhausted from trying to live up to everything she thought a mom was supposed to be. There will be more screaming, yet this time it's from your wife and not the baby. Yes, this is all going to happen to you. So enjoy the silence when you get it. Embrace it. Lean back in your easy chair and catch up on your sleep. Hug your wife and tell her that you love her and that she's a great mom. You are a team that must work together. You must put the chalk on the chalkboard and run plays together. It's 4th down and 1, and you've got to get over the goal line together to win the game. If you can do this, you'll enjoy the quiet moments you still have as a couple. Maybe you'll even get something better than silence...a quickie. Now that's my kind of happy hour.

Preggo-Stat temperature: LOW

She's showing and everyone wants to touch her belly. This might annoy her or she might encourage it. In either case, she's getting a lot of attention and happy about it.

Week 23

Break Time

My wife is always looking for a break – a reason to sit down, put her feet up, and relax for a bit. She deserves it. She's carrying around a bowling ball all day, every day, and you're not. The difference is that we're all looking for a reason to relax for a few minutes and unwind. Everyone carries their own kind of stress each day, but the difference is that you'll never get a break from raising children.

Kids make you tired. Very happy, yet very tired. I've learned to live on about 1.5 hours less sleep than I used to. I get up earlier than I used to and stay up later than I used to. Once the kids go to bed at around 7:30, you need to take some time to unwind. This is your time to sit down on the couch, watch some football, and crack open a cold one. You wish. Unfortunately, this will not always be the case. This precious two or three hours in the evening is now filled with last minute chores and tasks for you to get done. And now that you're wife is pregnant, she's going to milk this time as her down time and not yours. You'll have more trips to the kitchen only to realize that the dishwasher needs to be emptied again, even though you just emptied it last time.

While we're on the dishwasher subject, not only will you find that you're loading and unloading it more lately, you'll also be told that you don't load the dishes correctly. Women seem to have a secret dishwasher loading technique that men have not been able to crack. Women have been given some kind of special knowledge about proper plate and glass placement, as well as how much rinsing is needed before each item is placed into the dishwasher. At this point, my pregnant wife should just be happy that I'm doing it with a smile on my face, yet this is another pregnancy right of all pregnant women.

Enough about the dishwasher, as you'll be taking on many other household chores than you may already do, and you'll just find yourself doing them more than normal. This could be laundry, or maybe it's preparing dinner, or it might even be cleaning the entire house. The reality is that your beautiful wife is pregnant, and she needs a break. You'll hear this over and over and over again. And so many of my wife's sentences will start with, I just need to do this, or I just need a minute to do this, or I just need to lie down for a few seconds, or I just need a quick back rub, or I just don't have time to do that. So guess who gets to do it...yeah, you. And you'll do it with love, because you love your wife, and she's pregnant with your child. So get up early, go make some money, and consider your car ride home your break.

Preggo-Stat temperature: LOW

She naps daily when she has the chance, so she's too tired to beat you up. If you need a night out with your buddies, this would be a good time to do it.

Week 24

Register for Baby

Now that you're entering the third trimester, if you haven't registered at your local baby store, now's the time. Friends, family, and co-workers are going to be asking where you're registered and if they can throw a baby shower for you and your wife. Your house will soon be filled with more gifts than you've received in the last 20 years of your life. You'll be asking yourself how a little human being that comes into this world at about 20 inches long, and weighs around 8 pounds, could ever need so much stuff. I don't get it either.

Yet, somehow I found myself down at Newborns R 4 U mega-store on a Saturday afternoon with 1000 other crazy soon-to-be parents zapping baby items with a laser bar-code scanning gun to fill up our registry. This process will seem familiar as you probably registered for your wedding at some large department store, and filled your house with china that you'll never use, along with the bread maker and deep fryer that is collecting dust in your kitchen somewhere. Well, this will be much the same. You'll register, people will go and buy you stuff, it will take over your house, and then you'll be storing it all in your garage in case you have another baby.

How did we get to the point in life where you feel like you need a storage unit for all of the junk you collect in your house, but don't want to get rid of (or your wife doesn't want you to get rid of)? My wife has so many Christmas decoration storage bins that she could give Santa's workshop a run for its money – that's a completely different topic. Where the hell and why the hell do we keep all of this crap? I'm constantly going to Goodwill to drop off stuff or giving useless things to friends and neighbors, but the problem is that other friends, neighbors and family are constantly trying to give me their junk in return. It's like a big cycle of exchanging garbage I don't want anymore for garbage you don't want anymore!

Anyway, so we're at Newborns R 4 U. My wife led the battle through this mega-store like a general leading the infantry through enemy territory, gunning down all that stood in the way. She grabbed the scanner gun from me and tagged eight different kinds of pacifiers, four different kinds of bottles, and eight different kinds of nipple attachments for the bottles in one big swooping scan! I held the nipple attachments up to my chest and danced around, waiting for a cheap laugh.

Even the best gunslinger out there would be impressed with her skills, and we're only in aisle 1 of this 30-aisle warehouse of baby, baby, and more baby. I said, "Nice shot – it's my turn now." I grabbed the scanner gun back and tagged six rubber ducks for the bath, eight different styles of washcloths, and four types of baby bath wash. She looked at me, impressed; yet I was no match for her machine-gun-like tactics in this warfare. I handed the scanner gun back to her and watched as she worked her magic. Aisle 3, blankets, aisle 5, diaper bags, aisle 7, 8, and 9, bedding; this place is bigger than Costco!

And finally we get to the stroller aisle. Or should I say stroller lot. It was like a car dealership. Couples walked around, pushing, or test driving each stroller, kicking the tires, checking out the accessories, and then returning it to its parking spot. There were 12 different brands, each with 2 or 3 different models and styles, different colors and prints, and each folded up small enough to fit into a car trunk.

My wife pointed out that I might need to take my golf clubs out of my trunk just in case I need to put the stroller in it from time to time. I quickly countered with the statement, "Yes honey. And you'll need to take the knife out of my back, because that's about how your comment felt to me." Take my golf clubs out of my car? I usually stop off at the range a couple of times each week after work and hit some balls. My wife replied, "You won't have time to stop and hit golf balls on the way home from work anymore. I'm going to need more help at home now with the new baby." She was right. Yes, I'm sure I'll still have the opportunity to fit in the driving range every now and then, but my priorities in life are changing and I'll need to adjust my activities. Besides, I think most of these strollers will fold up small enough to fit in my trunk with my golf clubs.

I quickly stepped over to a metallic black-framed stroller with solid navy blue seating. "I like this one honey. It has three cup holders, a music and cell phone holster, a large basket area for holding blankets, and yes, a seat for the baby." She took it for a test drive, came back and said, "It's nice, yet the color is a bit plain for me." I said, "Remember, we're having a boy. Black and navy blue are excellent colors for a boy. When approached at the park there will be no confusion if the stroller is navy blue and he's wrapped in blue blankets." She wandered off to another stroller a little further down the lot. It was beige and a light green in color, and the framing was silver. "How about this one," she said. I was not impressed with the colors, but after pushing it around, I liked how it handled. It could turn on a dime and had some mini-shocks around the wheels for a smooth ride. I asked, "Does this come in blue?" "No," said Kelsey, the 16-year-old girl working this part of the lot. We kept looking, sipping our non-fat mocha-chinos, as we searched for the perfect stroller.

We folded, unfolded, pushed, pulled, debated on color, print, make, model, and size until we found one we both liked. It had two cup holders, a universal holder for a music player and cell phone, a couple of quick zip pockets for baby gear, as well as a large basket to put blankets and a diaper bag. The baby seat could be used universally with the car carrier seat, and on it's own with a baby tray when our little guy was bigger. It had a metallic black frame and solid red seating that made it look as racy as a 911 turbo. It also folded up flat enough that I knew for certain it would fit in my trunk alongside my golf clubs! I kept that part to myself.

Preggo-Stat temperature: MEDIUM

She's noticeably bigger and none of her old clothes fit. Her feet hurt and she'll ask you to rub them every night. Do it, or you'll be on her black list and the moodiness will elevate to high!

Week 25

Beer Run

By week 25, it's obvious my wife is pregnant. She's not a big, fat cow (week 36 – 38 she'll be a beautiful big, fat cow), but she's wearing pregnancy clothes now and wobbles a bit at times when she walks. People want to touch her belly and talk about when she's due. Everybody loves a pregnant woman, as she has a glow in her face that seems to radiate an inner peace and contentment about the life she is carrying inside that belly. Remind her of how great she looks now going into her third trimester, and definitely don't mention the fat cow thing. Always lead with a compliment if you're going to ask for something, right?

Well, I did just this while we were sitting in the car deciding who was going to go into the grocery and pick up a few items. She said that she would go in alone instead of sending me in with a list. I told her how great she looked, gave her my loving husband smile, and asked her to grab one thing for me. "Honey, could you also get me a 12 pack of micro-brews." She looked back at me and said, "If you want beer, go in and get it yourself!" What, I can't ask her to pick something up for me? I can't even tell you how many times over the years of our marriage that I've had tampons, tampons, and more tampons on my "honey do" lists. I've picked up sanitary napkins, toilet paper, diapers, condoms; you name it…I've been sent out for it. I've faced the checkout lady and looked her in the eye and then gone through an uncomfortable silence as she rings up my loot and packs it all in bags for me. This awkward glance continues as the clerk meticulously reviews the receipt to make sure I got the discount on the tampons my wife sent me to get. I go through the humiliation because that's what good husbands do.

Why will she not go through the same checkout lady stare for me? Why do I give, give, and give, only to be thrown the pregnancy card because of this one little request? As the beer goes down the short conveyor and the check-out lady looks up at my wife with those judging eyes, why can't my wife just take one for the team and suffer the same sort of uncomfortable silence like I have to endure? Well, she doesn't have to. Remember, you don't know diddlysquat about being pregnant. She's the referee in this game and gets to make all the calls. I didn't ask her to buy me a couple of cases of beer for my Sunday afternoon NFL tailgate party. It seemed like a reasonable request. But just like oral sex, it's not on the agenda anymore, so get out of the car you lazy jerk and get what you want yourself.

She came back to the car with the groceries, and smiled at me with a look in her eyes that said, *don't even ask me if I got you beer, you moron.* I didn't ask her anything. If I were her, I would find some humor in buying beer while pregnant. I'd maybe even make a comment to the check-out lady like, "Good sale today on beer...looking forward to sitting down and watching the game this afternoon." But hey, that's just me. If I ever get pregnant, I'll have to remember that one when I'm at the grocery.

Preggo-Stat temperature: HIGH

Your wife either loves being pregnant by this time or hates it. Both bring about elevated hormone levels. If she's overly happy, she'll drive you crazy with "honey do" lists. If she hates pregnancy now, she'll blame you and your penis. This will lead to even less sex. Not good.

Week 26

Just for Men – Paternity Leave

Paternity leave is becoming more common in the workplace for men. If your employer is going to give you 10 – 12 weeks paid time off, you are one lucky son-of-a bitch. You'll have time to play golf, hit the gym, catch up on some good books, clean out the garage, and still be there for your wife and new baby. Bullshit. You'll be so tired from the demands of your new routine that you will be begging to go back to work!

If your employer does not graciously offer you 10 – 12 weeks of paid paternity leave, you'll have to figure out different arrangements. You may be offered a week or two away from work, paid or not paid; yet it's important to take some time off to absorb being a new dad.

I did not have the option of full paternity leave with our first or second child. With our third, I did have the option of paternity leave, yet it was not fully paid. I work in sales, and my clientele is my source of income. Due to the nature of my work, I took off three weeks, which seemed like a sufficient amount of time.

I focused on the little things. I spent all day with my kids and our new baby. I gazed into their eyes to see the innocence that children have before the big, bad world takes them over. I embraced these feelings and vowed to carry them into the next chapters of our lives. My wife enjoyed having me take more time off with this baby, as it gave her more time to take naps!

I used to think that taking three months off was reserved only for those with a vagina. Why the hell would a man take three months off? How much work could a baby be? Well, it's a whole lot of work. Sleepless nights, spit-up all over your clothes, poopy diapers that leak, crying, screaming, and feeding this cute, little thing, can beat you up. If you can get three months off from your employer for paternity leave, take it fool. You'll need it.

Preggo-Stat temperature: HIGH

Her back hurts from the additional weight. She walks like a weeble-wobble, and her feet still hurt. She can't sleep well at night. If you've got the bucks, splurge for a pregnancy massage for her. If not, tell her how beautiful she looks, and you might drop the moodiness down to medium.

Week 27

Couples Baby Shower

Yesterday, my wife came to me about her baby shower. I was sure that one of her friends would be throwing it for her, and I'd be asked to help set up. Not quite. While she had planned to have a traditional baby shower given by a good friend or family member, she sprung a new one on me. She said, "Hey honey, how about we do a couple's baby shower?" I said, "Never heard of it, and I don't see why any guy would want to come to it." She said, "Well, we could have it later in the evening, get some drinks, play games, and make it more of a social event." I'm a bit more interested at this point, yet still waiting for the hook. The more I thought about it, the more I thought what the heck. Any excuse to get together is always good with me.

As it turns out, a couple's shower is when the men are invited too. The guys hang out and drink beer, make margaritas for the guests, and eat all of the food. The girls exchange baby gifts, talk about how long and hard the pregnancy has been, and trade stories about being a mommy. My wife told me she would incorporate some games for us men to play in addition to the typical baby shower stuff women do. After a few drinks, I'm good for about anything, so I agreed to it.

You'll find that your social life will soon revolve around baby showers, baby and children birthday parties, and just your baby in general. I am now a permanently programmed husband by my wife. She downloads the calendar into my brain and I am then able to exist. Any events that I need to accomplish are attached or planned around the schedule my wife has given to me. If I need to stop at the hardware store, I do it after I drop one of the kids off at a birthday party. If I need to go to the gym to workout, I do it later in the evening after the kids have gone to bed. If I need to take a shit, I do it with the realization that my wife will probably be yelling at me to hurry up because I need to pick up one of the kids from a play date. So if having a couple's shower is what it takes to drink some beers with my buddies, I'm down with it!

On the day of the shower, I started to wonder if this was really a good idea. I could have had some friends over for a NFL football game, or maybe I could have worked in a night of poker with the boys instead. This baby shower thing was starting to sound a bit soft. Yes, I'm excited about having a baby. Yes, I have a sensitive side to me that a man is not supposed to express. Yes, I am a caring, supportive husband. Yet I can't help but wonder if I just got trapped into a night of goo-goo gaa-gaa baby talk over tiny onesies and cute little diapers. Well, in a way I did...but the party games, drinks, and laughs made up for it.

The key to a good couples shower are the games. We had a fairly tight group of friends attend ours, so after a few drinks, everyone loosened up a bit. We decided to revert back to our college days and include a game called, "I Never." We then went on to a dad's competition that involved us guessing what chocolate candy bar is in each diaper (imagine a *Snickers* bar smashed up like poop and having to smell it). We ended with a few light-hearted, traditional baby shower games for the girls, and then it turned into a regular party. Sounds a bit adolescent, yet when you're married, have kids, or are expecting, it doesn't take much to liven up the evening. You see, everything right now is planned around the kids and baby. Anytime we want to go out, take a vacation, or just do it, we have to plan around the kids and baby. A few old drinking games brought back some spontaneity for us all.

We started off with the game, "I never." An example phrase to the game would be one of the ladies saying, "I have never given my husband any oral action while he was driving." If you have, then you take a drink. If you haven't, then you don't take a drink. Here's another -- "I never had sex with my wife while other people were watching." Surprisingly, most everyone took a drink on this one. The stories were flying about morning sex, doing it at the movies and at the office. Many were in swimming pools, hot tubs, or just bangin' it out in a spare bedroom at a party while another couple was also in the room. Wow. This wasn't the baby shower I was expecting!

The best story was what position do you think you were doing it when you made your baby? First, we had to narrow it down to the day or night when we thought conception happened. Then we had to recall what positions were used and how many times we did it that night. Some couples thought it was doggy style, while others thought it was an elevated missionary position that got the sperm swimming. Now that's something to write down in the baby book!

Everyone had a lot of good laughs, and the party transitioned into the traditional baby shower for the ladies, with gifts and cake. A few friends had to go home early to relieve their babysitter, while many stayed to have a couple more drinks and catch up on old times. After everyone left for the evening, I gave my wife a hug and thanked her for talking me into a couple's shower. I highly recommend it.

Preggo-Stat temperature: LOW

Your wife may or may not have had a baby shower yet. Her stress level should be low, as she's excited to visit with friends and family and go goo-goo gaa-gaa over new baby gifts. When the baby kicks inside her, she laughs and takes pleasure in being pregnant.

Week 28

Two-Hour Shower

The last few weeks my wife has complained about not having time to take a shower. "I haven't showered in three days," she says. Or, "I haven't had time to take a shower since last weekend." I reply, "That's just nasty. How can you not have time to take a five-minute shower?" She says, "Well, between shuttling our two kids to kindergarten and pre-school, play groups, and running errands, I just don't have the time. On top of that, I have to find time to rest with this pregnancy!" She has plenty of time to take naps, so why not just shower instead of taking a nap? I'm a problem solver, that's what I do!

She didn't appreciate that last comment, and proceeded upstairs for her Saturday ritual of a two-hour shower. After she awakes on Saturday morning around 8 a.m. (keep in mind I've been up since 6:30 with the kids), she comes downstairs to say good-morning. She gets to sleep in because she's the pregnant one and I'm not. Afterwards, she says, "I'm going to take a shower, honey." I reply, "Okay. I'll get breakfast going and be down here with the kids."

Her shower routine has become much more than a shower. It's her hall pass, which really means - don't bother me while these bathroom doors are shut, or I'll kick you in the nuts! She's going to go upstairs, shower, put on a mud mask, light some candles, maybe even take a bath after her shower, shave her legs, blow dry her hair, and so on. What the hell is this about? I'm downstairs with the kids going crazy, and she's upstairs in a two-hour spa treatment.

Her idea of taking a shower is much different than mine. If I were to be in the shower for over five minutes, the kids would be running into the bathroom, banging on the shower door, and asking when I'm going to be done. When I'm in the bathroom, how come she doesn't keep the kids out or put the do not disturb sign up for me? It's because that's another one of her pregnancy rights and it only applies to her. She gets to take personal time for herself and use it against me. She thinks that I have personal time Monday through Friday when I go to work. Ha! This is not personal time – It's time at work where my clients yell at me, my boss stresses me out, and I have to sit in traffic to and from that hellhole. I'd rather be at home with the kids!

The fact is, both our days are stressful in there own way. Unfortunately, her day will always be harder than mine. Now that she's pregnant, hypersensitive, and crying for no apparent reason at times, it doesn't matter what my day is like. Hers will always be harder. I try to remember this during pregnancy, even when she becomes the erotic emotional roller coaster she has been lately. Go take your shower, lock the bathroom door, and I'll see you around brunch time honey!

Preggo-Stat temperature: HIGH

Once she gets the baby shower gifts home, she realizes that there's much to do and so little time! Your wife is starting to nest. She's neurotic and barking orders at you like a drill sergeant. Hide in the bathroom.

Week 29

Nesting

The weekend started off fairly normal. I got up with the kids, she came downstairs and announced that she'd be taking a two-hour shower, and later I'd hear about how her back hurts and she's tired. After her nap, she awoke with her eyes wide open. "Honey, we need to get the baby room done this weekend!" she shouted. Uh oh – It's here...nesting!

Someone call 911, because the baby room is not done! The house needs to be childproofed again, and we need to pack our bags for the hospital. She went on and on and on - "I need to finish washing all of the baby clothes from the baby shower, buy diapers, reorganize the kitchen for baby bottles and accessories, plan out the schedule for when I'm in the hospital, arrange travel dates and times for family that wants to come and stay with us from out of town." I said, "Are we going to do all of this today, or can we take a few weeks to accomplish everything?" She said, "A few weeks - is your head stuck up your ass? We don't have a few weeks, you moron. I could have this baby any day!" I said, "Wow. All of that swearing is turning me on! How about a quickie before we get started?" She replied, "You don't remember anything. We can't have sex because of the Placenta Previa, and we don't have time for a quickie. I'm nesting dammit!"

I spent the greater part of the day painting the baby room and putting together a closet organizer. I also pulled the crib out of the attic. As I put the crib back together,

I started to get a bit sentimental. This might be the last time I assemble a crib. This would be our third child, and my wife said that I'm going straight to the vasectomy doctor afterwards. It's not that I disagree with my wife; it's more about realizing that this chapter in our lives is about to be over. And now that I know we're done having kids, it's different this time. The crib seems to be more than a crib. It's a moment in time that is finished and about to pass by. I love being a father, yet now that my "making babies" days are through, it's hard to imagine this crib going to a garage sale a year or two from now. As much as my wife is diving me nuts over these nine months, I wouldn't trade it for the world.

I can hear my wife shuffling things in the laundry room. Then the sweet, kind words of a pregnant woman echo down the hall, as she yells, "I'm going to be up all night doing laundry! You are making dinner tonight honey. I have things to do!" I shout, "Yes honey. I'd love to make you dinner tonight." Do I really have a choice? Chances are she'll be walking around the house organizing every nook, drawer, and cabinet all night long until she's satisfied.

As the weekend zooms by, outside of hanging up a few accent pictures, I manage to nearly finish the baby room. My wife finished the laundry, re-organized the kitchen, and made a list of the other ten thousand things that we have to do over the next week. She's on a mission and will not rest until all is done. I'm an innocent by-stander caught in rush hour traffic, just trying not to get hit by this bus. She's driving out of control for the greater good. Our little baby needs the house turned upside-down, cleaned twice over, and my wife is the one to do it. Watch out – nesting patrol is on duty!

Preggo-Stat temperature: HIGH

She's pissed off that you haven't finished all of the nesting projects she asked you to do. Help her get organized for the baby or you'll be sleeping on the couch.

Week 30

I'll Cry if I Want To

Today I called my wife just to see how the day was going. Hi, how are you, have you gone to lunch yet, how are you feeling, and so on. About half way through the call, she starts crying. What did I say? Was I listening? Did I miss some trick question and answer it wrong? I'm known to do that, as I tend to type e-mails, do paperwork, or attend to whatever else is on my desk when she calls. Sometimes she'll hear the click, click, click of the keyboard, and yell through the phone, "Type no sex for you until you stop and listen to me!" Ok. Got it – I'll stop typing. But this wasn't that at all. She's my crazy, emotional, pregnant wife and now she's crying to me on the phone in the middle of the day!

I ask her what's wrong. What happened today? She replies, "Oh, it's nothing. I'm just this huge blob and I have so much to still do before the baby gets here." I say, "I'm here to help honey. What can I do?" She says, "Next time, you get to have the baby! I want this thing out of me. Now!" I know that this is a trick question – I can answer it with factual knowledge, meaning it's impossible for me to have the baby. Or I can answer it with sensitivity. Such as, "I'd do anything for you honey," and I'd still be throwing her a bone for a beat down. Both answers are wrong, because she's a psycho pregnant woman with the right to cry as much as she wants for nine months! So instead, I just sit and don't say anything. At the ten-second mark, she says, "I'm sorry honey. I'm just really emotional right now." Now that she's admitted to giving me a ticket to riding the emotional crazy train, I realize that this ride still has about two months left. She tells me to have a good day, that she loves me, and the phone call is over.

By the time I get home, she's already in her pajamas lying on the couch watching a movie. I ask if she's craving anything for dinner and that I'll get it going. The crying starts again. Did I miss something? What movie was she watching? "Honey, what's wrong? I said I'll make dinner tonight." She says, "I know you said you'll make dinner. That's not it. I went up to my closet, looked at all of my clothes, and realized that I'll never fit in them again. I'm a big, fat pregnant lady, and will never fit back into my skinny jeans."

This is going to be a tough one. I think I'll try and just sneak out of the room. Maybe she won't notice me as I tiptoe around the corner to the stairs. Just as I start to make my move up the stairs I hear, "Honey, did you hear me?" I reply, "Yes dear. I heard you, and I know you'll get back into your skinny jeans again. You just feel that way right now." What was I thinking? I just fell into her trap! She yells, "Oh, so you think I'll be a fatty if I can't get back into my skinny jeans?" She starts crying more, throws a couple of pillows my way, and raids the tissue box to blow her nose.

What the hell just happened here? I'd like to give her a hug, but she'd probably kick me in the groin. I'll take my chances and try and hug it out. I say, "Honey, come over here. Give me a hug. I'm here for you." She walks over, lays her head on my shoulder, and says, "I'm sorry honey. I'm just really emotional right now." No shit! One minute I'm offering to make dinner for you, and the next minute you've trapped me like a helpless insect in your crazy, emotional pregnancy web.

After dinner she smiles and thanks me for making her favorite pasta dish, with garlic bread of course. She offers to clean up, so I'm going to change into my gym clothes and go for a run. Bad idea. I come back downstairs with my running shoes on, and she starts crying again. She says, "How come you're trying to get in shape while I'm pregnant? Are you trying to make me feel even fatter than I am? You should be gaining weight too. You should be gaining sympathy weight."

Even though I'm not having the baby, she thinks I'm supposed to put on 20 pounds just to make her feel better? I'm so confused right now - let me the hell off of this ride. Before I say anything, a few thoughts run through my head. One, I can't have sex with my wife because of the Placenta Previa condition (by now it might be hard to have sex anyway because her belly is so big). Two, I'm not supposed to exercise. Three, I'm supposed to put on sympathy weight. Four, she cries and screams at me for just breathing. Wow. I'm really in deep do-do here. I say, "I'm not really exercising. I'm going down to the grocery store to get some chips and ice-cream, and then eat myself into a state of pregnancy unconsciousness." She stops crying and says, "Thank you honey. That's the answer I've been looking for."

My Crazy, Pregnant Wife!

Preggo-Stat temperature: HIGH

The crying and sobbing are filled with mumbled words you can't understand. She may also be getting hemorrhoids. She's a train wreck waiting to happen, so stay clear of the tracks.

Week 31

Leveraging the Baby Excuse

Last night I got a phone call from an old college friend. We talked for a bit, re-lived the past glory days of beer bongs, fraternity parties, and waking up in the morning with one of your eyebrows shaved off. We had mutual friends in the dorms, and the evenings would turn into a game called, "Beers from around the World." Each dorm room would be labeled a country, and the beer or drink served in that dorm room would have to be from that country. We would wander from country to country" saturating our liver in alcoholic beverages from around the world. There was one evening in which I was so drunk that I peed into the closet in my dorm room while I was sleep walking.

I couldn't remember anything about the preceding night when I woke up the next morning. The only proof of the event was the damp floor and the smell of urine on dirty clothes at the base of my closet. Yes, I was a chic magnet. Girls love the smell of liquid body waste lingering in a dorm room, right?

After reminiscing for half an hour, this old college buddy states that he's coming back to the area and wants to know if during the next weekend I could help him move in. Help him move? I hate it when people ask me if I can help them move. It's a friend trap – no one really wants to help anyone move. People do it because they feel like they have to. When someone asks you to help him or her move, you'd rather have the excuse of going to a funeral. At least then you could just sit on your ass in church instead of breaking your back lugging hide-a-bed sofas up two flights of stairs to your buddy's new loft.

Right before I was about to say yes, I blurted out, "I'd love to, but my wife is pregnant and due soon. We have a hospital tour set up for Saturday, and I'd be in the dog house if I missed it." The hospital tour was legitimately scheduled for Saturday afternoon, and it was structured to enable expecting parents to come in and visit the birthing rooms and ask questions about the big day.

My buddy replied, "No problem. I hear you on that one." I replied, "Yeah. Otherwise I'd be right there helping you. I'll try and stop by afterwards." After I got off of the phone I realized that the baby excuse would be coming in quite handy for many things in life. Don't want to go to an annoying co-workers dinner party...baby excuse. Don't want to go to a friend of a friend's birthday party...baby excuse. Don't want to go to your neighbor's swinger's party...baby excuse. This is awesome. I can regretfully decline about any invitation to any event with the baby excuse.

Friday night – you'd rather rent the latest James Bond flick and plant your ass on the couch with the wife: "I wish we could make it over for dinner Friday night (at the house of that annoying couple who always want you to stay up all night playing board games), but we have to keep the baby on a strict eating and sleeping schedule for the next few months."

Saturday afternoon – you'd rather be watching baseball: "I know you could really use the help painting a couple of rooms, yet I can't be around paint fumes and bring them home to the baby."

Sunday morning – you'd rather be at home in your pajamas watching the pre-game football show: "I really wish we could be there. Now that we have the baby, it's going to be hard for us to make it to your daughter's church choir program. But we'd really like to go if we could."

Your wife will be able to use it too. She'll quickly learn the leverage of the baby excuse.

Friday night – she'd rather put the baby to sleep, rent the latest chic flick, and hit the couch with you: "I'd love to go out for ladies night (and be your sober driver while you puke in my car), yet I'm still nursing and need to lay off the alcohol for a few months."

Saturday afternoon – she'd rather run errands, go the grocery, stop by the mall, and grab a late lunch with you: "Hi Marcy – You have extra tickets to your volunteer organizations fundraiser? Wow, wish we could make it, but the baby is crying quite a bit of later and I wouldn't want that to ruin your fundraisers' luncheon."

Saturday evening – she'd rather be watching you watch the Lakers game: "You're having another purse party? Wow. Didn't you just have a jewelry party last week (where she spent $300.00 on toe rings and "energy" bracelets)? I'd love to make it, yet I'm just not ready to leave our baby for the evening."

Now you can both turn down any event in life with grace and still seem completely genuine. We all have these little events in life that we feel like we have to attend. It's the right thing to do. But now, you have the baby excuse. It's been used on us in the past, and now the torch has been handed to my wife and me once more!

Preggo-Stat temperature: LOW

The crying has stopped and she's sane for the week. Enjoy it by going over to a buddy's house and having a few beers. You'll need friends to talk to and help you get through the pregnancy.

Week 32

Complication Revisited

Earlier today we visited another doctor to get a second opinion on the Placenta Previa. My wife does not want to have a c-section, yet if the Previa does not correct itself, she'll have one for the safety of the baby. Its visits like this that remind me of how much my wife's body has taken on over the last seven months. I'm reminded of how fortunate we are to have a healthy baby up to this point.

I take my wife's hand and reassure her that all will be fine, and in just weeks we'll be celebrating the arrival of our little boy. She smiles at me, yet anxious to hear what the doctor has to say. She says, "Why is he taking so long to get the results?" I reply, "Take a deep breath. You've done everything that you can, and now you just have to let the last few weeks happen, regardless." She squeezes my hand tighter.

The doctor finally knocks on our little waiting room door and enters with his clipboard and file in hand. "Hello," he says. As he runs through the results, it's again non-conclusive that the Previa has corrected itself. It's now a marginal Previa, and it still may or may not correct itself before labor starts, which means that a c-section can't be ruled out. My wife starts to tear up. She wants a yes or no answer. She's still nesting and trying to organize the rest of her pregnancy, including the birth plan. Unfortunately, this is a plan that has a plan of its own. Life has a plan of its own. I give her a hug and hold her tight, pushing my waist out in order to accommodate her growing belly.

For now we'll have to take it week by week as she begins to have more appointments during this last month. I can only think positive that the Previa will correct, and we'll be able to have a natural birth. If it doesn't, we'll have to adapt for the safety of the baby and for her too.

Although this has been a minor complication up to this point, any complication in pregnancy leads you to thinking about the worst-case scenario. I'm trying to avoid that, as I'm a "glass is half full" kind of person. I reassure her that it's not a complication. It did not get worse – it just hasn't corrected yet. If we're patient, life will work itself out just as planned. I take her hand again as we walk out of the office. "I love you," I say. "I love you too," she replies.

Preggo-Stat temperature: HIGH

The sane week was short lived. She might be leaking milk from her boobs. It's called Colostrum. She continues to be uncomfortable at night and could start having Braxton Hicks contractions. Pick up the pregnancy book and talk about the next few weeks together. You're only a few weeks away from the big day!

Week 33

My Empty Wallet

I went to a web site this morning that calculates how much it is going to cost to raise a child. The costs ranged from $355,000 to $426,000. This covered all of the basics, like housing, food, transportation costs, clothing, healthcare, early education expenses, as well as college expenses. Wow. I guess we should have just got a dog. My wallet feels like it already has a big hole in it, and we haven't even had the baby yet.

Even as I sat there staring at the computer screen, this cost seemed a bit low. By the time this kid is 18, college expenses alone could be $200,000. Ouch! Now I'm really having a coronary. How the hell am I going to pay for this? What if my wife changes her mind and wants four or five kids? I might as well buy a large life insurance policy and hope for an early death. When I gave these numbers to my wife to look at, she gets that same look on her face that she makes when I accidentally break wind when she's still in the room. Disgusted, yet not surprised. She says, "Well I guess you can kiss early retirement goodbye." Then she adds, "If the baby was a girl, we'd be paying for part of the wedding too." Nice. I'm already saving 50 grand because we're having a boy. Somehow I'm supposed to be comforted by that comment. She doesn't seem overly concerned and goes back to folding baby clothes in the nursery. I better get some child labor out of this kid, if he's going to cost me half a million dollars to stay at my house!

Preggo-Stat temperature: HIGH

Your wife is retaining water and waddling more when she walks. She's nervous about all of the "what-ifs" that the next few weeks may bring. What if the baby comes early? What if I start bleeding? What if I must have a cesarean section? These are all questions the both of you should talk to your doctor about. Use the doctor to calm your wife down and help out with the anxiety and pressure of the last few weeks.

Week 34

Milk Me

Today I met my wife at the doctor. Our doctor said that it's now safe to have the baby. Week 34 is still considered pre-term, yet outside of any other health issues, this stage tends to be just as healthy as full-term. My wife's response was, "Great. Get it out of me!" Our doctor chuckled and informed us that there was no reason to induce at this point, so she should "cook" her little bun in the oven a bit longer.

We went out to dinner after the appointment. We had Italian, as she's still craving spaghetti and garlic bread much like she was earlier in her pregnancy. While we were sitting there eating, I noticed that her shirt around her boobs was wet. I asked her about it, and she told me that her boobs were leaking milk. Then I said, "Oh, you mean like a cow?" She replied, "Yes honey; like a cow. I am now a farm animal with milk leaking out of my boobs; hemorrhoids on my fat cow ass, and my feet are retaining water like a big fat cow. Why don't you reach over here and milk me."

I was trying not to laugh. I actually thought it was kind of sexy. I even told her that, but it didn't help. Her reply was, "You think doing it with a cow is a turn on? Do you think that I want to lie there while you play out some farm animal sex act? You're sick." I was getting nowhere with this one. I had dug a deep grave with the cow comment. I told her again that I thought it was a turn on, and her wet, milky boobs were making me horny. Again she replied, "I'm not having sex with you. You'll have to live out your milk fantasy in another lifetime. We can't have sex anyway because of the Placenta Previa."

I sat there in silence while we finished dinner. I played the silent game with her, but finally broke. I said, "Hey honey. I'm sorry about the cow comment. You're beautiful, and I love you." She smiled at me, reached for my hand and said, "If you ever call me a cow again I'll grind your dick up into ground beef." Ouch. I smiled at her and said, "Speaking of dicks, we're going to have our little guy circumcised right?"

Preggo-Stat temperature: HIGH

Her body is physically exhausted by the end of the day. The cute little baby kicks inside her belly have now turned into annoying movements that cause her more pain. She wants to strangle you, so watch your back.

Week 35

Kick the Tires

This weekend is our hospital tour of the maternity ward. I woke up excited, thinking about some of the action we might see and hear. We were also scheduled to take a newborn CPR class afterwards.

I could already picture doctors running up and down the stale white hallways, women screaming from inside each closed door of their birthing rooms, and nervous dads holding video cameras at all of the wrong angles to document these timeless moments on tape. I was finally going to get a glimpse of the excitement I was anticipating on our big day.

To make the day more exciting, I thought it might be fun to use this trip as a practice run – kind of like a dress rehearsal for the big show's opening night. And just to make it a bit more real, I packed her a small duffle bag full of overnight clothes. All along I didn't tell my wife about any of this.

Our appointment for the tour was to start at 10 a.m. My wife came downstairs at 9:30 and said that it was time to go. I jumped up from the couch and said, "Honey, did your water break? Is it time to go to the hospital?" She looked at me dumbfounded and said, "What are you talking about? This is our hospital tour." I walked over to her and said, "I know sweetie. But let's pretend this is the big day. I'll go get your bag, you get in the car."

She played along, seeing the humor that I was getting from it. I grabbed her stuff, ran back down the stairs, and jumped in the car. Now it's time to set that land speed record to the hospital.

I tore out of the neighborhood, with my wife yelling at me to slow down. Yes, this is just how I imagined it. She's screaming, I'm driving faster and faster, and we should be there in less than ten minutes. With every green light that I make, another 30 seconds is shaved off of my time. I round a curve with the precision of an Indy-car racer, and then punch it down the straight a way. If a cop were to pull me over now, I'm sure he would understand and later lead me to the hospital with his lights on like a pace car bringing me down the home stretch.

Another green light...yes! "I'm not driving dangerously, just offensively," I tell my wife. She begs to differ. "Slow the F down!" she yells. I again tell her, "Honey, I'm being careful. I've driven these roads many of times. In fact, I know side streets and short cuts in case there's an accident blocking our route." She says, "You're crazy." Well, I might be a bit crazy, but it's in her best interest. I don't think she'd want to have the baby in the car, so it's best that we get to the hospital as fast as we can. That's what I'm here for.

We pull into the parking garage and find a spot right up front. I pull in, park the car, and look over at her and say, "9 minutes, 25 seconds." She looks at me in disapproval, yet I can see a smile emerging from the sides of the evil eye she's giving me. I knew I could make it in less than 10 minutes, yet now we're 20 minutes early for our tour.

We make our way over to the hospital maternity ward, and I'm ready for the fireworks. We get off of the elevator, it's completely silent. There are no doctors running up and down the hallways, no screaming moms yelling at their husbands, and all of the babies are asleep in their little cribs behind a big glass window. I look over at my wife and say, "Are you sure this is where you're actually going to give birth? I see babies, yet it's too quiet, and all of these doctors and nurses look way too calm. This is not at all like I pictured it." She took my hand and we walked over to the front desk to register for the tour.

The nurse walked us down the hall to see some of the birthing rooms. Most were quite large, had a window, a fold out bed for the dads, and a private bathroom. There was also a TV, DVD player, and mini-fridge. "These rooms remind me of one of my old dorm rooms," I said. We later saw the nursery, family waiting room, and directions on how to find our way to the hospital cafeteria. The nurse took us through all of the equipment, including the birthing bed, which had all sorts of things attached to it. She fielded questions from our tour group and left us with a folder full of additional hospital information to read--and complete. Afterwards, we walked by the nursery one more time to admire the little babies sleeping.

I left a bit disappointed. I wanted to hear the energy of babies being born. I wanted to hear women screaming from their rooms as they tried to push a small watermelon from their vagina. I wanted to see dads giving each other "high-fives" in the waiting room. I wanted to hear newborns yelling at the top of their lungs as they gasped for that first breath of air. I didn't see or hear any of this. I told my wife, "I guess we came on a slow day." She leaned over to me and said, "Well, it wasn't a total bust. You did set a new land speed record to the hospital." And that I did.

These final few weeks will eventually bring our big day. My wife has some pretty big lungs on her, so I'm sure I'll get plenty of screaming and crying recorded to document the arrival of our new little baby.

Preggo-Stat temperature: MEDIUM

Your wife is extremely uncomfortable, and may be having light contractions or Braxton Hicks. Her feet are swelling more and she may need different shoes for additional comfort. Be on high alert for comments like, "I don't think I could ever do this again." Or, "Next time, you get to have the baby." These are all signs that the large cantaloupe that she's carrying between her legs is starting to become unbearable. Be strong, you're almost there!

Week 36

Visitation Rights

Today I got a call from my mom about their visit once the baby is here. My folks live out of state, while my in-laws live in state. My mom was asking me about possible dates to come and visit once the baby is here. Within the next few weeks we'll have more company come through our house just to catch a glimpse, and maybe even hold this little baby, than we've ever had before. With that, my wife has instructed me of visitation rights for friends, family, and the others.

The grandparents obviously come first. There's no stopping them. Whether you want them in your house or not, they are coming over. As helpful as they can be, at times you'll find you may need an exit strategy.

Next on the list are brothers, sisters, and other extended family members who may want to come by. All of your family (except for that crazy uncle in the family) make up you're "A" list. You'll be counting on these people in the future for babysitting, advice, support, and more babysitting.

After that you drop to the "B" list, which are your friends. I often refer to these people as the real "A" listers, as you'd like to replace much of your family with your friends. This group actually listens and will be a part of your life, versus your family who prefer to talk at you and offer advice when it's not asked for. You can pick your friends, and you can pick your nose, but you can't pick your family...or something like that.

Next are the "C" listers, which are the others: neighbors, acquaintances from church, work, or any other outside affiliation that each of you may have. The great thing about "C" listers is that they often bring food. Anyone that brings food automatically gets bumped up to the "B" list for future visitation rights.

My wife gave me her proposal of the post-birth schedule. It goes something like this. She offers up some five days for my parents to visit and stay with us after the birth. I counter her proposal with two extra days, upping it to a total of seven days. She re-counters and accepts my offer with the contingency that I talk my dad into helping me finish a couple of handyman projects around the house. I accept.

She then proposes her parents schedule. She'd like her mom at the birth, family to visit at the hospital, and then a three-day break before they visit us at the house. I accept with the contingency that if they do drop by during the three-day break, they must bring us dinner. She accepts.

As we talked more about the visitation schedule for "B" and "C" listers, it became apparent that the main concern was sleep. It wasn't that we didn't want to celebrate this glorious event with everyone involved in our lives. It was that we'd be tired as hell. She'd be recovering from the birth long after the two nights and three days that she would spend in the hospital. I'd be tired from waking up every two hours to help my wife change, feed, and rock our baby back to sleep. Much of our sleep and rest would come during the day when our baby sleeps. Therefore, if we had constant company dropping by, we'd be even more sleep deprived.

Sleep becomes harder and harder to get with kids. Eventually you adjust, but that first time around can be a killer. You'll fight over who gets to take a nap or who's going to get up with baby all night long. Even if you come up with a schedule for days or nights on who will get up at night, one of you will always end up with more or less sleep than the other. Get over it. No one gets to sleep when there's a newborn in the house. As far as I'm concerned, anyone who brings over food when they visit moves up the list. Even that crazy uncle in the family that no one talks about.

Preggo-Stat temperature: HIGH

Her shoes don't fit anymore. When she stands up, she can't see her feet. When you look at her belly, you can see the baby's movement, which seems to be throwing elbows into her ribs. She passes gas unexpectedly and doesn't care. You should be scared, so put on her favorite movie and throw a bucket of popcorn in her lap. As long as she's eating something, she can't yell at you for the pain you've given her.

Week 37

I Sat Down and I Can't Get Up

She's in meltdown mode today. Her feet hurt, she's cramping, ankles are swollen, and you can see our little guy doing somersaults in her belly. This baby is active. Not a minute goes by that he's not elbowing, nudging, and kicking her in the ribs. Contractions are coming throughout the day, yet not long or far apart enough to go to the hospital. We were told that the contractions should last about a minute and come every five minutes for about an hour. Ask your doctor what he or she believes would require a visit to the hospital.

My wife has called her doctor about five times so far today, and it's only noon! The office tells her the same thing after each call. "Yes, your contractions are still too far apart, so just breathe and call us when they get much closer." I think I heard her talking to the receptionist about which room she preferred when she did go into labor. Unfortunately, I don't think the maternity ward works like a hotel. "Yes, I'd like a room with a view of the mountains, corner suite if possible, and do you have room service?" You do get room service, yet it's from the hospital cafeteria, which holds down a solid 1 out of a 5 star rating. Try the meatloaf...you can never go wrong with the mystery meat rolled into a loaf.

After the last phone call she yells upstairs to me, "Honey – bring me more pillows, and when you get down here, I'm hungry." I yell back, "Sure thing sweetie. Anything you need, I'm here for you," I'm a short-order cook these days. Just yell out what you want, and it will be delivered fresh from me to you on the couch.

After I throw together a 5-course lunch consisting of 2 grilled cheese sandwiches, a side of macaroni salad, potato chips, an ice-cream bar, and a 32-ounce lemonade, she's feeling better. Thinking it is safe, I head back upstairs to finish a couple more things in the baby room.

Five minutes later, she yells up to me, "Honey, we're out of toilet paper. Can you bring some down?" How could she already be done with lunch? I guess she pounded that lemonade like tequila shots on spring break. "I'll be right down honey," I say. Right before I walk around the corner to the bathroom, I hear ffffffffaaaaaaaaarrrrrrrrttt! She's still gassy. I started to chuckle a bit, and held my nose as I quickly tossed in the toilet paper roles. She said, "Get over it. If you haven't noticed, I'm pregnant." I left before the reconstituted smell of grilled cheese filled the air. "I'm going back upstairs to finish a couple of things in the nursery," I said.

Not more than two minutes later, I hear her crying...then she's laughing, crying, and laughing again...what's going on? I run back downstairs and she's still sitting on the toilet. I also ran into the lingering stench from earlier. I breathe through my mouth, trying not to inhale, and ask, "What's wrong, honey?" She looks up at me and says, "I sat down and I can't get up." She starts laughing again, and then crying as tears come down her face. She goes on to tell me that she has a cramp in her leg, and her feet are so swollen that it hurts to put the needed amount of pressure on her heals to stand up.

I reach down to help her up, and then quickly say, "Wait – I need to take a picture." She yells at me, and I quickly reply that I was just kidding. I help her back up, like a 90-year-old woman that has fallen in the kitchen. She leans on my shoulder for a minute after she stands up. I whisper in her ear, "Honey, you need to pull your pants up." She looks down not realizing that she forgot to pull her pants back up. She's officially hit rock bottom in the pregnancy journal. I walk her back to the couch and she asks if I can rub her feet for a bit. I tell her that I will as long as she gives me fair warning of any eruptions caused by grilled cheese still lingering in her system.

Preggo-Stat temperature: HIGH

You'll be constantly interrupted with her wants and needs all day. Your only chance of any down time is if she takes a nap. Encourage napping as she needs the rest, and you need a break from being her servant boy.

Week 38 – 40

My Water Broke, Run Dad Run

I came home early from work today. It was a Friday afternoon, and I was ready to get the weekend started. It was a sunny spring day, and while I drove home on a congested freeway, I thought about how I could be getting "the call" at any moment. I checked my cell phone to make sure the signal was strong. It was. I wanted to be sure I was there right away if my wife's water broke or her contractions got so close that we needed to rush to the hospital. I checked my phone again. The ringer was on loud, and the signal was strong. I'm all good.

I got home to find her resting on the couch. She was surprised to see me, gave me a hug, and upstairs I went to change out of my suit. Seeing that I was home early, I thought I'd go for a jog. I know what you're thinking...how dare I exercise at this point in my wife's pregnancy. I'm supposed to be gaining pregnancy weight with her. Well, I decided that I'd binge on junk food and pregnancy cravings with her, yet still exercise. I went downstairs, gave her a kiss, and said I'd be back in about an hour.

I ran down our street and led myself over to my usual jogging trail just outside the neighborhood. It was a great trail that took me through open fields, up a couple of hills that brought grand views of the lower valley, and then back around to a man-made trail of bark dust that wandered along a protected green-belt. It was about a seven-mile loop that I could take a short cut on and reduce to five miles if needed.

As I jog along, my mind drifts into another world. I always exercise with music. It motivates me and takes me away from all of the other thoughts that would otherwise consume my head. As I drifted into a 60-minute music mix of 90's alternative rock bands, I felt so alive. This was my time. This was my alone time. This was my 60 minutes that could not be interrupted by screaming kids or a nagging wife. I was in the zone.

I decided to make it a five-mile loop today and turned off early to head back home. As the trail ended, I stopped to walk and cool down at the entrance to our neighborhood. I came around the corner to our street and saw my wife standing out on the driveway waving her arms furiously in the air. What the hell was she so worked up about? I ran down the street and finally heard her voice screaming, "My water broke! I've been standing here waiting for you for over 15 minutes!" "Holy shit! We've got to go to the hospital now," I said. I ran in the house to get her things and couldn't find them. "I can't find your overnight bag," I yelled to her. She replied, "I've been waiting here for 15 minutes. I've already put my bag in the car. In fact, I could have re-packed my bag and drove myself to the hospital by now, so get out here and drive!"

Dripping in sweat from my run, I thought I'd jump in the shower very quickly just to get the smell off of me. She heard the shower turn on and yelled at me, "Are you in the shower?" I quickly turned it off, jumped out and dried myself off. "No honey – I'm just changing my clothes." I ran downstairs and she could see my wet hair. As she glared at me I said, "I was all stinky and sweaty from my run. I just needed to wash off." She was nearly ready to punch me. Gritting her teeth, she said, "I'm about to have a baby. I'm going to be sweaty, stinky, and making nasty grunting sounds as a small bowling ball squeezes through my vagina, and you're the one worried about taking a shower right now?" She's got a good point. I left it at that, smiled, rubbed her belly, and held her hand as we walked to the car. "I love you honey," I said. "I love you too," she replied, and now it's time to have a baby.

We tore out of the neighborhood, set another new land speed record to the hospital, and rushed up to the maternity ward. As we explained that her water broke while I was out for a run, the nurse looked at me and said, "Why didn't you take your cell phone with you?" While I appreciated her feedback on the situation, jogging with a cell phone is not the most comfortable thing to do. I replied, "Yes, yet I would still be jogging on a trail and would not be able to get back any faster than I did." While the nurse and I debated the logic of this predicament, my wife interrupts and says, "Excuse me. I'm going to have this baby right here on your front desk counter if you don't get me checked in ASAP!"

After signing in, they take us back to run some tests, check her contractions, blood pressure and so on. I held onto her hand and said, "We're going to have a baby!" As the excitement builds, the nurse comes back in with the results. We're told that even though her water broke, she's only dilated to three inches, and her contractions are still over six minutes apart. Normally they would send us home at this point, yet because her water broke, she'd be admitted. In other words, it could still be a while before the rest of her body decided to shoot out the baby.

Even though our excitement was diminished a bit, the fact that we're this much closer to having our little guy come out of her body still brought chills to my spine. We're in the bottom of the ninth inning, bases loaded, and my wife was up to bat.

It was 6 p.m. on a Friday. We'd moved into our maternity-ward suite. It had a TV, DVD player, mini foldout couch for me to sleep on, and a view of the mall across the street. Her bed was lined with pillows that could be placed in all kinds of different locations to make her more comfortable. After she changed into the lovely hospital gown, the nurse helped her into the bark-a-lounger bed. It had a remote to move the mattress into multiple positions. My wife got comfortable in the bed, and now we wait.

We waited, and waited and waited. It was now 10 p.m., and still no action. Her body just wasn't ready yet. Family had come and gone for the night and asked that we call as soon as she was in labor. This wasn't anything like the evening I thought we'd be having. I was prepared to have a baby by now and we weren't even in official labor yet? My wife's body may have not been quite ready, yet emotionally she was ready. I looked over at her and said, "Well, maybe we'll get a night's sleep and you'll have the baby in the morning?" She looked at me and was about to say something, when her body suddenly tightened up and she let out a long screech. "Yeeeeeeeeeeeeeeeeoooooooooooooowwwwwwwwwwww," she screamed, sweat starting to form on her brow. We both looked up at screen that monitored her contractions. It was a 5.0 on the Richter scale. Now this is the kind of labor I pictured!

The nurse came in and said she had just paged her doctor. Ten minutes later her doctor came in and did a quick check. She had dilated to four. Our doctor said, "This is it guys. Are you ready to have a baby?" She also told us the good news that she felt the Placenta Previa had corrected, and she'd be able to have a natural birth! My wife was so happy. She didn't want to go through a c-section, along with the additional recovery that a c-section required. That alone made her worries go away, and now she was in the zone.

We called my wife's mom, and she came up to the hospital that evening to help out. We decided to have her in the room with us during the birth for extra support. She could help sooth some of the aches and pains that come with labor as only a mother can.

At around 1 a.m. her contractions started to level off and she hadn't dilated any farther. It might be a bit longer than our doctor had originally predicted before the baby came. She told us that they would like to start a treatment that induced her a bit, which would move her labor along quicker. The doctor also asked if she'd like an epidural for the pain, but my wife opted for all-natural childbirth. She'd be regretting that in about two hours!

At about 1:30 a.m. I stretched out on the pullout couch that was there for the dads to sleep on. Within about ten seconds I had fallen asleep. I woke up at 3:30 to screaming. Oh damn! Did I sleep through the birth? As I sat up, my wife screamed again. Her contractions were closer together. She looked at me and said, "Did you enjoy your nap, honey? I'm over here in excruciating pain and you're sleeping!" I jumped up, grabbed the camera and said, "Smile honey."

For the next three hours my wife rode out her contractions, eagerly waiting for the baby to come shooting out of her. She said, "Why hasn't this baby come out yet, and tell the nurse to get in here and give me some drugs! You did this to me, and next time you get to have the baby!" She had officially hit her threshold of pain, and I was to blame. I said, "Okay honey. I'll go get the nurse."

The nurse came back in and said that it was too late for an epidural. She was too far along. Her doctor came back in to perform another check. It was now 6:30 in the morning. She said, "This is it guys. Are you ready to have a baby?" My wife looked down at her and said, "I was ready eight hours ago when you said that!"

By now there are three nurses in the room, the doctor, my mother-in-law, and me. It's a sold-out show. As I pulled my wife's hair back out of her face, I kissed her and knew that the moment was almost here. "I love you," I said, "I love you too," she replied. As she pushed for the next few contractions, my wife's scream was suddenly over-taken by another scream. It was the scream of our new baby boy! Our doctor quickly wrapped him up and placed him on my wife's chest. Sweat dripped down her face as she glowed with tears of happiness that only childbirth can bring. I'll never forget the feeling of pure, innocent joy that fills that one finite moment in life. It is absolutely amazing. Nothing can describe the level of emotion that takes over your senses as you see and hear your newborn gasp for that first breath of air. I am a blessed man, husband, and father too...life is wonderful.

About the Author and Acknowledgments

The author, Jeff Walter, is inspired by humorous conversations found in the everyday life of family and friends. He lives in Southern California with his wife and three children. Nothing gives him more joy than spending time with his family.

Special thanks go out to my wife, who might say that I am the one that is crazy. With her love and support, I was able to finish this book with wild imagination and dramatic tales of living with my lovely pregnant wife.

27921650R00100

Made in the USA
Middletown, DE
26 December 2015